Abiding

in

Messiah

Bearing Fruit in Yeshua

Abiding in Messiah

by Miriam Nadler

© 2011 by Miriam Nadler
All Rights Reserved
Printed in United States of America
ISBN: 9781519294708

Table of Contents

FOREWORD 4

MY TESTIMONY 6

THE SONG OF MY BELOVED 11

SPIRITUAL WARFARE 43

ABIDING IN THE BELOVED 63

A LIFE OF SIGNIFICANCE 89

BIBLIOGRAPHY 114

RESOURCES BY WORD OF MESSIAH MINISTRIES 116

Foreword

Yeshua asked Peter, "Do you love me?" He asks this same question of each of us today. Do you love me more? More than the world, more than yourself, even more than your life. But how can we love Him? By bringing Him glory through abiding on the vine. In this study we will consider how to stick to Him like glue, thereby bearing much fruit. This book is written from a Messianic Jewish frame of reference. Therefore, we will use Messianic terms such as *Yeshua*, which means Jesus in Hebrew. We also will look at some key Hebrew words with the hope that it will deepen your understanding of the Scriptures.

I am thankful first and foremost to Yeshua for His eternal commitment to me, for being my Vine and for never giving up on me, His little shaky branch.

I am especially thankful for my friend, Natalia Fomin. Natalia was a continual source of encouragement as we worked together to see this project completed. Her friendship is truly a gift from the Lord and a confirmation of how God can use us to make a difference for eternity as we seek to honor the Lord with our lives. Natalia is truly a woman of excellence!

I pray that you will not only be blessed by reading this book, but that you will also be motivated to bear good fruit, hence being the cause of much heavenly rejoicing.

In His Love,

Miriam Nadler

My Testimony

uring my college years as a very young believer, I was discipled by Arnold Fruchtenbaum, who is a Jewish believer in Jesus and now leads Ariel Ministries. For some reason, Arnold saw in me ministry potential, even though I was basically immature and untaught in the Scriptures. As he discipled me in aspects of the faith, like believing God to provide for my school bill as I worked my way through college, he also gave me an understanding and love for the Jewish people. He encouraged me to write my papers for English and History on various aspects of Jewish life, especially the Holocaust. I became involved in Arnold's prayer group for Israel, and the Lord put a burden on my heart to reach out to Jewish people.

I spent four summers ministering in Brooklyn, New York with Hilda Koser, who was one of the great Jewish missionaries for Messiah. As I worked alongside her during the summer Bible school outreaches in Coney Island, NY, Miss Koser taught me how to minister to children.

The Lord provided another mentor in my life: Ruth Wardell. She was a Gentile believer in Messiah who made a profound impact for the Lord among Jewish young people.

As a counselor at Camp Sar Shalom for Jewish teenagers, I watched Ruth interact with them. With her example and encouragement and by God's grace, I was able to have a positive impact on the lives of a number of young women as a camp counselor and Bible teacher.

After graduating from Cedarville University with my degree in teaching, I knew that the Lord was calling me into Jewish ministry. I taught for a short time in public school to pay off my college bills then moved to New York City to work with *Chosen People Ministries* (then the American Board of Missions to the Jews). I moved to New York City with great joy and anticipation because I knew that the Lord was leading me.

During my first six months in the city, I studied under Moishe Rosen, who later started *Jews for Jesus*. I immersed myself in Jewish culture, learning the Hebrew language and Israeli music. I began a small women's Bible study. We met every Friday night on the Upper West Side in the building that Chosen People Ministries then owned. I would often cook a meal, where about a dozen ladies would gather to study and be discipled. This was my first experience of teaching a women's Bible study, and I was certainly a novice. I was only 21 years old, and some of the women were twice my age.

After three years of ministry in New York City, I had the privilege of moving to Israel, where I studied at Hebrew University in Jerusalem for a year and took some post graduate courses. I also studied Hebrew at an *ulpan*, which is an intensive language school. But that year in Israel turned out to be not merely a time to study but a time to minister. Through one on one friendships and a coffee house outreach in Jerusalem that I helped to start, I had various opportunities to share my faith. After my year of study and outreach in Israel, I moved back to New York City.

Later the Lord led me to move to California to help start *Jews for Jesus*. When we began a music team called *The Liberated Wailing Wall*, I met a new believer named Sam Nadler. In chapter two I will tell the story of how we met. The Lord definitely brought us together in love and in ministry.

For the first few years of our married lives we were on the road, crisscrossing the USA doing concerts for both evangelistic outreach and to raise support. Eventually our touring days ended, and Sam and I moved to New York City. We began our outreach work there by opening the New York branch of *Jews for Jesus*. I started discipling women one on one and in small groups.

In 1979, God called Sam to provide leadership for *Chosen People Ministries* (CPM), which he did until 1996. As CPM's NYC Director, Sam first mobilized the staff to engage in team-oriented outreach that was bold, creative, and culturally relevant. This served to enhance the ministry's local profile and evangelistic productivity.

Along with raising our two sons, Josh and Matt, I served alongside of Sam who had become Northeast Regional Director for CPM. Convinced that the

Great Commission meant evangelism that produced discipled believers, we began personally planting as well as supervising the planting of several Messianic congregations in the Northeast US. As God's blessing on our ministry became evident, Sam was asked to lead the worldwide organization in 1989.

As President of CPM, Sam brought new strategic intent to the global work. With the Great Commission as his objective, Sam launched the century-old Jewish ministry in a new strategic direction: the planting of Messianic congregations among the Jewish people. When Sam and I began *Word of Messiah Ministries* in 1997, we wanted to concentrate on helping to build up congregations through practical discipleship materials.

Today I am blessed to have an opportunity to disciple women and develop teaching materials to build up and encourage women in their spiritual walk.

For Messiah's Glory,

Miriam Nadler

Let me sing now for my well-beloved a song of my beloved concerning His vineyard. My well-beloved had a vineyard on a fertile hill. He dug it all around, removed its stones, and planted it with the choicest vine. And He built a tower in the middle of it and also hewed out a wine vat in it; then He expected it to produce good grapes.

(Isaiah 5:1-2)

Chapter 1

The Song of My Beloved

God's Vineyard

*H*ave you ever thought of God as a romantic God? If He invited you to His vineyard that He designed with His own hands, would you be excited to spend time with Him there? Take a journey with the Beloved to His vineyard, a romantic place with luscious grapes hanging from the vines. In Isaiah 5:1-2 we find a description of the wonderful provisions God has given to His vineyard so that His vineyard would produce good grapes. God was expecting Israel to bring forth excellent fruit.

As we consider why our Beloved has left us here on earth instead of taking us home to be with Him, we need to understand that our lives are to be lived in light of His eternal provisions because He is expecting each of our lives to produce good grapes.

One of the purposes of our lives as believers in Messiah is to point those around us to our Beloved. The lives that we touch should be drawn to consider a relationship with God through our fruit—to see His beauty, hear of His wonderful works, smell His sweet aroma emanating from our lives and thereby have the desire to "taste and see that the Lord is good."

The *Song of My Beloved* is also called the *Parable of the Vineyard*. A parable is a story that teaches a spiritual or moral lesson and throughout this parable there are three characters that are noted: Isaiah, His Beloved, and the nation of Israel. As we take a closer look at this song we realize that the singer of this parable is the author himself, Isaiah the prophet. When I think of Isaiah, I think of a man who was a great orator for the Lord. In Scripture, a prophet represents God to people by his spoken words, but in this section, Isaiah is a singing prophet. Perhaps Isaiah was trying to get the attention of Israel in a new creative way since they were not listening to his strong oratory. Perhaps Israel would listen to a poetic song.

THE ART OF COMMUNICATION

It has been said that women have a knack for communication. Like Isaiah the prophet, in our roles as mothers, teachers, wives and friends, we are always trying to communicate our needs and our desires through creative behavior, in ways that will bring response. When my two sons were younger, instead of yelling at them about the need to take out the garbage, I decided to leave a note on the fridge with a smiley face: "Don't forget to take out the garbage!" And it worked, they responded positively without the constant nagging. Another example: when my husband Sam was pressed for time as he prepared for an overseas ministry trip, rather than just affirm my love and support verbally, I would place a card in his luggage so he would find it sometime during his journey. This note was my way of letting him know of my love and care for him that would encourage him as he was ministering. Isaiah begins, "Let me sing now for my well-beloved a song of my beloved concerning His vineyard. My well-beloved had a vineyard on a fertile hill" (Isaiah 5:1). Who is the beloved that is mentioned three times in the first verse? Isaiah is singing about His God, the God of Israel. Isaiah is not just singing about an impersonal force of nature or a creator who did not care about his creation. Rather, this Beloved is someone who loves personally and who cares about what He has planted.

A HILL OF STRENGTH

Next we read where Isaiah's Beloved has planted His vineyard. Verse one states that this vineyard is planted on a very fertile hill. The word "fertile" in Hebrew is actually a phrase *ben shemen* which literally means son of oil or son of fatness. This soil was not just any old piece of dirt, but it was His soil with His oil that would produce the lush fruit He desired. We not only have the soil mentioned, but also the location of the vineyard. He was planting this vineyard on a hill, which is the Hebrew word *keren*.

I was surprised to see this word *keren* in this verse because it is more commonly translated horn symbolizing strength or might. I was familiar with this word *keren* from my studies of Hannah.

In 1 Samuel 2:1, we find Hannah beginning her prayer of thanksgiving using this word *keren* or horn to denote the source of her strength.

> 1 Samuel 2:1 —And Hannah prayed and said, "My heart exults in the LORD; my horn (*keren*) is exalted in the LORD, My mouth speaks boldly against my enemies, because I rejoice in Thy salvation."

In Isaiah 5:1, the word horn is translated as hill, which is another meaning for the Hebrew word, *keren*. The Beloved of Israel is planting His vineyard in the best location, on a hill, a place of strength. In fact, it was essential for a fruitful vineyard to be in the right location because grapes need a sunny place to grow and thrive.

The vine needs to have the sun shining on every part of it, in order for the grapes to mature into luscious fruit. This vineyard provides the ideal location in the perfect soil. For us as well, when we become the beloved of God through a personal relationship with Yeshua, we are planted in the rich soil of His promises and provision. In Isaiah 61:3, there is a promise to Israel that will be fulfilled by their acceptance of what Messiah alone can give. We, who are trusting in God's provision, can also experience the promises from Isaiah. It says in Isaiah 61:3,

> To grant those who mourn in Zion, giving them a garland instead of ashes, the oil of gladness instead of mourning, the mantle of praise instead of a spirit of fainting. So they will be called oaks of righteousness, the planting of the LORD, that He may be glorified.

REMOVING THE STONES

Messiah is not only the source of the oil (*shemen*) of gladness, but He is also the source of all light that we need to grow and flourish. Yeshua proclaimed to the crowd in the Temple in Jerusalem, "I am the Light of the world; he who follows Me shall not walk in the darkness, but shall have the Light of life" (John 8: 12).

Isaiah 5:2 gives us a more detailed description of what our Beloved is doing for His vineyard.

> Isaiah 5:2 —And He dug it all around, removed its stones, and planted it with the choicest vine. And He built a tower in the middle of it, and hewed out a wine vat in it; then He expected it to produce good grapes, but it produced only worthless ones.

First of all, the Beloved of the vineyard digs all around the area to be planted and removes the stones that are there. The Lord is removing the obstacles that would hinder the growth of the vines. Since the soil in Israel in many places can be very rocky, the removal of stones is necessary before any planting can begin.

CASTING OUR CARES ON HIM

We learn from the song that God has the power to remove the obstacles not only from this soil spoken about here in Isaiah, but also from our lives. We need to trust the Lord and realize that He desires to remove all those things that will hinder our growth in Him. I know that many times I desire to mature in my walk with Him and glorify the Lord, but a rock of disappointment or anger will pop up in my life that can paralyze me and rob me of intimate fellowship with the Beloved. It could be a stone of grief or bitterness that is hidden in the soil of my soul. I may have buried it so deeply that I am not even aware that it is there. However, as God reveals the stones that are in my life, He then removes them. I can be confident His power is sufficient and that His gentle hands will heal my heart and restore me to fruitfulness. I also understand that I cannot remove these stones by my own effort.

Therefore, I must look to my Beloved who is not only able, but also desirous to remove these stones. In Psalm 55:22, we are told to "cast our burden upon the Lord, and He will sustain us." This idea to cast means to fling or throw away. As you throw the rocks of your life to the Lord, He will remove them and restore you. This should be a daily process in our walk with the Beloved.

The Psalmist understood the need to trust in the Lord day by day as he proclaimed, "Blessed be the Lord, who daily bears our burden, the God who is our salvation" (Psalm 68:19). Take a moment to think of any stones in your life and how they may be hindering your growth, then ask the Lord to remove them.

THE CHOICEST VINES

The next phrase, "choice vine" reiterates Israel's value to the Lord. This phrase comes from the Hebrew word *sorek*, which is used two times in the Old Testament. First in Jeremiah, where God is pleading with Israel to repent.

Jeremiah 2:21a —Yet I planted you a choice vine, a completely faithful seed.

And again in Isaiah 5:2, it says that the Lord Himself is planting the choice vine. This was to be the best vine planted in stone-free, rich soil.

Like the choice vine we are of immeasurable value to our Beloved. Yeshua assures His disciples that we are no longer slaves but rather His friends, His chosen, and His select vine. Messiah's own words to His disciples should encourage us as well.

> John 15:16 —You did not choose Me, but I chose you, and appointed you, that you should go and bear fruit, and that your fruit should remain, that whatever you ask of the Father in My name, He may give to you.

PROTECTION FROM PREDATORS

Now God tells His people through Isaiah's song that He will not only plant them, but He will also protect them. Notice that our Beloved built a tower in the middle of the vineyard. Why would He need a tower? This tower is a watchtower for the vinedresser, and pictures the protection and refuge that God can give.

> Proverbs 18:10 —The name of the Lord is a strong tower, the righteous runs into it and is safe.

Since the tower would be in the center of the vineyard, the vinedresser could protect his vineyard from every side. How encouraging for us to think that the Lord is our refuge and strength, in Him we are eternally secure.

But why would the vinedresser need to protect His vine? Because there are predators that would seek to destroy the vineyard. Unless they are stopped, wild animals would come and steal the grapes preventing them to be used for their purpose. One of these predators that seek to destroy this fruit is a small animal called the fox.

THE VERY SNEAKY FOXES

Foxes are very common in Israel and they are particularly fond of grapes. They burrow holes around the gardens and unless strictly watched, would destroy whole vineyards.

Aristophanes, an ancient Greek writer, compares soldiers to foxes, because they consume the grapes of the countries through which they pass. These foxes represent anything that brings harm and destroys by stealth and cunning, the graces of those who are the objects of divine love.

Yeshua called Herod a fox in Luke 13:32 because he was an enemy of God's people.

The fox is mentioned in the Song of Solomon and it will be helpful for us to understand how these foxes could destroy the fruit that God wants us to produce.

> Song of Solomon 2:15-16 —Catch the foxes for us, the little foxes that are ruining the vineyards, while our vineyards are in blossom. My beloved is mine, and I am his; He pastures his flock among the lilies.

These verses teach that those who are favored richly with grace and love and who our Lord is drawing towards heaven, will be careful to guard against sins, especially little sins. Let us look at these verses in context.

The Shulamite woman wants to catch the little foxes— notice the phrase at the end of verse 15: "while our vineyards are in blossom." In other words, she knows that she needs to catch these foxes while their love is blossoming, so their love for one another will not be thwarted.

This Shulamite woman realizes there could be little irritations that could begin to destroy her trust and love for her beloved. She understands that her beloved is not going to be home until the evening. He needs to be away and will be back at the end of the day when his work is done.

> Song of Solomon 2:17 —Until the cool of the day when the shadows flee away, turn, my beloved, and be like a gazelle or a young stag on the mountains of Bether.

She could become impatient and complain about her beloved. Where is he already? If he really loves me, he would come home earlier and spend more time with me. What if he is really with another woman and not working late?

SECURITY IN THE BELOVED

Instead of allowing her thoughts to be corrupted, she declares her love.

> Song of Solomon 2:16 —My beloved is mine, and I am his.

Notice that she is assured and confident in his love for her. She is declaring, "I am for him and he is for me. We love and trust each other. It is mutual and I can trust in his love for me and love him right back." However there are "little foxes" that will constantly seek to erode her trust and her love. These little foxes can be seeds of distrust, complaining or even false teaching that will corrupt the heart and mind.

In Ezekiel 13, we learn that if a person keeps his mind fixed on false information or teaching, it will corrupt the heart of the listener:

> Ezekiel 13:3-4 —Thus says the Lord GOD, "Woe to the foolish prophets who are following their own spirit and have seen nothing. O Israel, your prophets have been like foxes among ruins."

We need to ask ourselves if there are little foxes that are spoiling the special relationships we have. This could be a relationship with your husband, a special friend or more importantly your relationship with the living God, your Beloved. A small fly can stink up the works, just as a little foolishness can lead to more foolishness. We learn in Ecclesiastes 10:1,

> Dead flies make a perfumer's oil stink, so a little foolishness is weightier than wisdom and honor—little sins beget the greater sin.

As wives, are we allowing little things in our homes to edify or tear down our families? Proverbs 14:1 tells us how to build up our homes,

> The wise woman builds her house, but the foolish tears it down with her own hands.

Another example of a little fox to watch are the small roots of bitterness that could begin to grow in our hearts (Hebrews 12: 14-15). We need to realize that small sins like a little leaven in the dough can lead to greater sins of pride and rebellion. David's prayer in Psalm 19:12-14 has become the prayer of my heart: Who can discern his errors?

Acquit me of hidden faults. Also keep back Thy servant from presumptuous sins; Let them not rule over me; then I shall be blameless, and I shall be acquitted of great transgression. Let the words of my mouth and the meditation of my heart be acceptable in Thy sight, O LORD, my rock and my Redeemer.

THE SHOCKING TRUTH

The next section of verse two tells us what God expected and what He received instead. Isaiah 5:2b says,

Then He expected it [the vine] to produce good grapes, but it produced only worthless ones.

Israel's Beloved was waiting eagerly for His good grapes, but to His disappointment he found nothing, but worthless fruit. Why? Because Israel trusted in themselves instead of trusting in the Lord, and therefore the fruit was worthless.

Rotten fruit is bad news! Many of us may be familiar with the phrase, "One rotten apple spoils the whole barrel." This means that a single bad influence can ruin what would otherwise remain good: A rotten piece of fruit can have widespread power. When I see those tiny fruit flies milling around a corner of my kitchen, I immediately check for any rotting fruit. Perhaps you have picked up a piece of fruit that looked really good, but when you bit into it, you were in for an unwelcome surprise! It was rotten!

For my life as well, if I am trying to produce fruit apart from depending on the Holy Spirit, then even though I may look good on the outside, the lasting fruit will be seen for what it really is. If I bear fruit apart from depending on the righteousness of Messiah, then it will be rotten.

Elizabeth George describes this idea in her book, *A Woman's Walk with God*:

> Throughout the Bible, the word fruit refers to evidence of what is within. If what's inside a person is good, then the fruit of that person's life will be good. But if it is rotten, the fruit of that person's life will be bad.

THE WILD GRAPES

The Lord was expecting good fruit, but instead found wild grapes. In Hebrew, the word for wild grapes (*beuseem*) literally means stinking or worthless. This fruit smelled terrible and was not good for anything except to be thrown out. This same root for this word is used to describe the stench of the dead fish when the Nile was turned to blood.

> Exodus 7:18 —And the fish that are in the Nile will die, and the Nile will become foul; and the Egyptians will find difficulty in drinking water from the Nile.

This repulsive odor (*beuseem*) was caused by God's judgment on the Egyptians for keeping Israel as their slaves.

This word for worthless or stinking also describes the condition of the manna that was kept over for an extra day against the teaching of God.

> Exodus 16:20 —But they did not listen to Moses, and some left part of it until morning, and it bred worms and became foul (*beuseem*); and Moses was angry with them.

This putrid manna came about because of disobedience to God's explicit instructions. Some of the children of Israel did not trust the Lord to provide for each day and felt they needed to hoard the manna.

THE STINKY FRUIT

David says in Psalm 38:5, "My wounds grow foul (*beuseem*) and fester because of my folly." In this Psalm, David is saying that his wounds have grown stinking and are festering because of his sinfulness or foolishness. In other words, this stench is a chastisement for his sin.

From these examples, we see that our fruit can be rotten for a variety of reasons: as a result of God's judgment upon us for treating Israel harshly (Exodus 7:18), for disobeying God's word and not trusting Him to meet our needs (Exodus 16:20), or by living apart from God's plan for us and suffering the consequences of our own foolishness and sin (Psalm 38:5).

The reason we are still here, on this side of heaven, is to bring honor to the Lord with our fruit. Whether it is the fruit of our lips or the fruit of our actions, the purpose is always to bring glory and honor to our Beloved. In verse four of the Beloved's song we can feel his frustration and concern for his vineyard.

Isaiah 5:4 —What more was there to do for My vineyard that I have not done in it? Why, when I expected it to produce good grapes did it produce worthless ones?"

ISRAEL'S FRUIT IS JUDGED

What happens when we decide to bear fruit apart from the watchful care of the Vinedresser? When Israel chose not to enjoy their Beloved's rich provisions and promises they faced dire consequences. They refused to depend on

God and produce good fruit. Therefore the Lord put them through the fires of testing.

> Isaiah 5:5-6 —So now let Me tell you what I am going to do to My vineyard: I will remove its hedge and it will be consumed; I will break down its wall and it will become trampled ground. I will lay it waste; It will not be pruned or hoed, But briars and thorns will come up. I will also charge the clouds to rain no rain on it.

God will take the following actions in response to their fruitlessness:

I will remove its hedge and it will be consumed - Remember the little foxes that want to spoil the vine? Without a hedge of protection the vines will be easy pickings for those foxes. God is removing their protection from predators.

I will break down its wall and it will become trampled ground. Cities have walls encircling them in order to secure their citizens from enemy attacks. Think of the city of Jericho from Biblical times. This ancient city was heavily fortified, with a virtually impregnable double wall that completely surrounded it. Walls were meant to protect the citizens who lived in the city.

And I will lay it waste; It will not be pruned or hoed, but briars and thorns will come up. I will also charge the clouds to rain no rain on it. God says that He will prevent His vineyard from bearing any edible fruit because the land will not be cultivated. There would be no pruning for this vineyard. In the place of luscious fruit, briars and thorns would grow.

In conclusion, God shows the power and might of our Creator God as He declares, " I will also charge the clouds to rain no rain on it." No protection, no pruning, no rain — is God overreacting to the fact that His vineyard will not bear good fruit? Think about the purpose of the Beloved's vineyard. He wanted to have intimate fellowship, drink the sweet wine, and enjoy His delicious fruit that reflected His character. Instead we read that He found bloodshed and a cry of distress. In verse 7 God reiterates the purpose for His vineyard.

> Isaiah 5:7 —For the vineyard of the LORD of hosts is the house of Israel, And the men of Judah His delightful plant. Thus He looked for justice, but behold, bloodshed; For righteousness, but behold, a cry of distress.

What was the rotten fruit that Israel produced? What did it taste like and how did it smell? There are six specific woes that are given in Isaiah 5:8-25. The word "woe" is a lament meaning alas, sadly, regrettably. In Hebrew this word woe is translated *oy* or *hoy*. Today *oy* is a common word in Yiddish. In the book *The Joys of Yiddish* Leon Rosten gives us further insight:

> Oy is uttered in as many ways as the utterer's histrionic ability permits. It is a lament, a protest, a cry of dismay, a reflex of delight. But however sighed, cried, howled , or moaned, oy! is the most expressive and ubiquitous exclamation in Yiddish. Oy vay! Literally means oh, pain.

In Isaiah 5 these *oys* are warnings from God's broken heart as He pronounces judgments on the specific sins of His people. We can understand His pain because the fruit of His beloved vineyard did not produce the desirable results.

He was expecting to see the reflection of His character in them instead they brought dishonor to His name.

Therefore they were reaping the harvest of their attitudes and their resulting activities since they were living for their own fruit and not the fruit of the Vinedresser. As we think about these sins let's evaluate and consider the kind of fruit we are producing. Let us examine the rotten fruit that our flesh produces apart from the Lord; apart from Him, we can never produce anything that would reflect His character.

COVETOUSNESS IS GREED

Isaiah 5:8-10 —Woe to those who add house to house and join field to field, Until there is no more room, So that you have to live alone in the midst of the land! In my ears the Lord of hosts has sworn, "Surely, many houses shall become desolate, Even great and fine ones, without occupants. For ten acres of vineyard will yield only one bath of wine, And a homer of seed will yield but an ephah of grain."

They have broken the tenth commandment of the law of Moses, which states, "You shall not covet" (Exodus 20:17). What does the word covet mean? Covet or *chamad* in the Hebrew means to desire, be attracted to, take delight, or find pleasure in.

The sin of covetousness is characterized by wanting more and more. However, this passage implies that they were not only coveting but also they were enriching themselves at the expense of others. Their covetousness was a result of their discontentment with what had been given to them as they desired to add another house and another field to their assets. God declares that their great effort to acquire more will actually yield them very little in return.

The apostle Paul in his letter to the Colossians equates this fruit of covetousness with idolatry (Colossians 3:5). We have to realize that when we covet we are in fact saying that God cannot supply all of our needs, which means that we are testifying that God is not omnipotent and all sufficient. We are not looking to the Lord, but rather giving into our yearnings of the flesh whether it is a craving for more things or different circumstances. What is it that you truly long for? Is it prosperity, family, fame, the noble peace prize? Or would you rather seek to serve the Lord with all your heart?

GOD IS OUR SUFFICIENCY

Our Beloved will not only meet our needs, but also will fulfill our hearts desires. There is nothing wrong with having desires. One of my favorite Scripture verses is Psalm 37:4, "Delight yourself in the Lord; and He will give you the desires of your heart."

In this Psalm King David is exhorting us to have our joy in the Lord and He will answer our prayers. In other words, as we yield our hearts to God and enjoy intimate fellowship with Him, He will bless us. Deuteronomy chapter 28 speaks specifically of the blessings the Lord desires to pour out into our lives. However, they are conditional and dependent on our obedience. If we will obey and listen to His word then the Lord will pour out His blessings. However, if we are not seeking the Lord as the Creator and provider we are looking to another source. Instead of bearing the fruit of answered prayer we will have little to show for our coveting and be unlikely candidates to be coveted by others.

EVERYTHING I NEED FOR THE JOURNEY

A few years ago, I began to travel regularly overseas for ministry purposes. My desire was to take lots of different clothes and as much luggage as I could, so I would be well dressed for any situation. I soon learned that is was much easier to travel light with just one carryon bag.

However, traveling light was something I had to learn. I had to give up my insecurities about needing to have a bunch of clothes and trust that I had everything I needed for the journey, with more than enough resources provided along the way.

The Apostle Paul encourages the congregation at Philippi to understand that believers can actually learn to be satisfied in any situation, "for I have learned to be content in whatever circumstances I am" (Philippians 4:11).

The Greek word for content means sufficient or having everything you need for the journey. Do you believe that God is your sufficiency and that He has provided all that you need for your journey of faith? *El Shaddai* is the Hebrew name for Almighty God. *Shaddai* is based on the root *shad*, a women's breast, and brings the idea of God pouring out all that we need. He is our sufficiency.

Philippians 4:19 —And my God shall supply all your needs according to His riches in glory in Messiah Yeshua.

Let us be thankful that we serve a God who is able to make all grace abound to us, that always having all sufficiency in everything, we may have an abundance for every good deed (2 Corinthians 9:8).

How does coveting or idolatry defame the character of God? Our greed for more drives us to idolize false gods and it states to the world that *El Shaddai*, the Almighty, All-Sufficient God cannot meet our needs.

THE SIN OF DRUNKENNESS

Isaiah 5:11-17 —Woe to those who rise early in the morning that they may pursue strong drink; Who stay up late in the evening that wine may inflame them! And their banquets are accompanied by lyre and harp, by tambourine and flute, and by wine; But they do not pay attention to the deeds of the LORD, Nor do they consider the work of His hands. Therefore My people go into exile for their lack of knowledge; And their honorable men are famished, And their multitude is parched with thirst. Therefore Sheol has enlarged its throat and opened its mouth without measure; And Jerusalem's splendor, her multitude, her din of revelry, and the jubilant within her, descend into it. So the common man will be humbled, and the man of importance abased, The eyes of the proud also will be abased. But the LORD of hosts will be exalted in judgment, And the holy God will show Himself holy in righteousness. Then the lambs will graze as in their pasture, And strangers will eat in the waste places of the wealthy.

In these verses drunkenness is portrayed as those who are so addicted to alcohol that they begin their carousing as soon as they wake up in the morning and continue through the night. As they pursue getting drunk, their only focus is to have more fun and frivolity thereby ignoring what is pleasing to the Lord. As a result there is severe judgment including: going into exile, drought, devastation, and humiliation. If they were continually drunk, looking for more amusement to fill their lives they would be living in a stupor, unable to even understand what is pleasing to the Lord because they did not pay attention to the Lord's provision and the works of His hands.

I can personally relate to the sin of drunkenness. My father, who has since gone home to heaven, was an alcoholic. As a young girl I remember how painful it was for me to see him drunk and in his state of inebriation. His condition would influence the whole household bringing sadness and frustration. When my dad was out of control he would do and say things that he later regretted. Please don't misunderstand my dad was a wonderful man who just wanted to escape for a while.

I would venture to say that most of you reading this book would not have a problem with excessive drinking, but perhaps you are pursuing activities and relationships that are dulling your mind and putting you in a stupor. You may be living your life looking for the next mirage to fill the emptiness of your soul.

A mirage is an optical phenomenon that creates an illusion of water. It is a distortion of light caused by alternate layers of hot and cold. To the naked eye, this illusion can look very real. However, the camera does not lie. If you try to take a photograph of what you believe to be real, when the film is developed, the illusion will not be in the photo.

Some of us may be allowing our disappointments, our self- indulgence, our emotional pain to lure us into a spiritual coma. We are vainly going after mirages.

BEING FILLED WITH THE SPIRIT

Scripture exhorts in Ephesians 5:18 to not get drunk with wine, but instead to be filled with the Spirit of God. This passage goes on to explain where we should focus our attention: speaking and singing God's word to each other and in our hearts, always giving thanks for all things in the name of Yeshua the Messiah. And to be in submission to one another as we give reverence to Messiah. If I try to fill my life with anything that is not pleasing to the Lord then I cannot serve my Beloved with my whole heart. Since we are instructed to be sober and alert, a drunken state will bring dishonor upon the God that we claim to serve. This drunkenness can lead to the next woe, which is carelessness.

CARELESSNESS AND MOCKING

Isaiah 5:18-19 —Woe to those who drag iniquity with the cords of falsehood, And sin as if with cart ropes; Who say, "Let Him make speed, let Him hasten His work, that we may see it; And let the purpose of the Holy One of Israel draw near And come to pass, that we may know it!

The sin of drunkenness leads to the sin of carelessness and mockery with those who are bound up in sin. How is sin seen in a careless lifestyle? Some synonyms of carelessness are: thoughtless, inconsiderate, unthinking, unconcerned, insensitive, and unsympathetic. I don't want others to treat me in a careless manner, rather I desire to be cared for, which implies: love, respect, concern, consideration, thoughtfulness, sensitivity and empathy for who I am, and also my particular situation.

The Israelites were so caught up in their sin that they carelessly mocked the name of the Holy One of Israel, not respecting, but taunting Him to perform His works. This particular name, the Holy One of Israel, is used twenty-five times throughout Isaiah's book and emphasizes not only God's character of holiness, but also the fact that God is the God of Israel.

All these judgments are being given in light of the fact that God is Israel's Beloved. He desired for the vineyard that He planted to bring forth fruit that would reflect His nature to the nations. However in this section we find these Israelites giving no respect for the name of God they were supposed to glorify. Instead they ridiculed and mocked the Lord as they continued in their sinful lifestyle.

HIS DUE WEIGHT OF GLORY

We serve a Holy God, the only One who is worthy of glory and honor. Both words glorify and honor are based on the Hebrew word, *kavod,* which means heavy or weighty. God desires fruit that will bring honor to His name, not dishonor.

We need to examine ourselves to see if we are taking the Word of God seriously, or becoming careless, thereby regarding His Word frivolously.

Sometimes when a difficult situation arises in my life whether it has to do with work or relationships, my initial fleshly response is to think to myself, "Well, I just don't care. I am not going to bother with this." Even though I realize that such an attitude is not godly, it arises from my need to guard myself. I want to build up a protective layer of hardness around my heart so I won't have to feel the pain of the situation that may unfold. But I believe that this attitude leads me to the sin of carelessness and that caters to my carnality. My focus is not on the Lord, but rather on thinking about how I can protect myself.

In a sense, I am becoming drunk with self-indulgence and if I allow myself to go into a stupor, I will not be able to care the way the Lord cares. A stupor or careless drunken state can result from any activity that takes your focus away from the Holy One of Israel and living for Him.

CREATIVE CARELESSNESS

As creative individuals we can find diverse ways to become careless about the things of the Lord. If we concentrate on anything without prioritizing the Lord, whether it is intellectual pursuits, sports, a career, the pursuit of wealth, or even good works, we will become careless about what really matters to God.

In my life when I try to protect myself from heartache I end up becoming insensitive to my Beloved, who is the only One who can truly protect and comfort me. Scripture exhorts us, "Seek first His kingdom and all these other things will be added to you." How do we desecrate the name of the Lord with our carelessness?

By taking His word lightly and not giving the Holy One of Israel honor. We need to give the Lord His due weight of glory so that the fruit of our lives will reflect His holiness.

THE SIN OF DECEPTION

Isaiah 5:20 —Woe to those who call evil good, and good evil; Who substitute darkness for light and light for darkness; Who substitute bitter for sweet, and sweet for bitter!

As we proceed down the list of *oys* or woes we see a progression as one sin leads to another, from greed to drunkenness to carelessness leading to deception. Deception is the sin of taking God's Holy moral principles and obscuring His values with double speak or making an euphemism for sin.

In other words, they were not admitting that sin is sin, but instead calling evil good, saying that darkness is light and replacing bitter for sweet. This behavior is abhorrent to God.

These deceivers of the Word were giving new definitions of moral standards. In today's society we have the same thing happening. For example, increased taxes are "revenue enhancements," and those who commit adultery are "challenged in marriage" and medical malpractice is not the cause of a patient's death; it's a "diagnostic misadventure of high magnitude."

In Psalm 12:2 these deceivers are described as lying to one another with flattering lips that speak from a double heart. The expression, "I'll do it my own way" is a euphemism for the sin of disobedience. When Saul disobeyed the Lord's explicit instructions what did the prophet Samuel say to Saul?

1 Samuel 15:22-23 —Samuel said, "Has the LORD as much delight in burnt offerings and sacrifices as in obeying the voice of the LORD? Behold, to obey

is better than sacrifice, and to heed than the fat of rams. For rebellion is as the sin of divination, and insubordination is as iniquity and idolatry. Because you have rejected the word of the LORD, He has also rejected you from being king.

From this Scripture we realize that those who disobey God and are rebellious to Him are practicing sin like divination and idolatry.

OUR GOD CANNOT LIE

In contrast those who follow the God of truth, serve a God who cannot lie, and those who practice dishonesty are emulating Satan, who is called the father of lies (John 8:44).

If we are in a stupor and become careless with the Word of God then it should not be a surprise that we would not understand the Holy principles of Scripture and begin to put our own adaptation to God's commands. We can quickly fall prey to the enemy of our souls and deceive ourselves and others. This is why we need to be students of the Word so we will understand the Scriptures and His Holy standard. John N. Oswalt comments:

> Sin can only be satisfied when righteousness is destroyed. If the ethical imperative is dependent upon human reason alone, that reason is no match for rampant self-interest. In fact, a prior commitment to the revealed wisdom of God (Proverbs 1:7, 3:7; 9:10) and a commitment to call good good, despite the reasonings of the wise of this world, can make possible genuine long-lasting righteousness both in individuals and in society. The path of those who chart their own course leads inexorably from self –aggrandizement to the ultimate reversal of moral values.

How does this fruit of deception disgrace the God of Truth? Messiah declares, "I am the Way, the Truth, and the Life" (John 14:6). When we lie, we defame God's character as we try to bring Him down to the level of the father of lies.

THE SIN OF PRIDE

The downward spiral of *oys* continues with the fifth sin of pride that is described in Isaiah 5:21, "Woe to those who are wise in their own eyes, and clever in their own sight!"

The deception leads to pride as it is seen in the leaders who thought they were so intelligent that they did not need to consult with God for His answers. How many times in my self-will do I forget to pray and just plunge ahead with my own plans? My carelessness that leads me to self-deception imitates the behavior of Satan. In Isaiah 14:12-15, we find a passage that explains the behavior of Satan and how he fell from his position as the chief archangel. Notice how many "I wills" are reiterated.

> How you have fallen from heaven, O star of the morning, son of the dawn! You have been cut down to the earth, You who have weakened the nations! But you said in your heart, "*I will* ascend to heaven; *I will* raise my throne above the stars of God, And *I will* sit on the mount of assembly In the recesses of the north. *I will* ascend above the heights of the clouds; *I will* make myself like the Most High." Nevertheless you will be thrust down to Sheol, To the recesses of the pit.

The "*I wills*" show Satan's true nature and motivation. His display of self-will and pride reflects his character and this fleshly self-rule is what our flesh desires as we emulate the evil one.

In our popular culture this idea of self-will is captured in Frank Sinatra's song, *I Did It My Way*. When I hear this song on the Golden Oldies radio station several Scriptures immediately pop into my head.

> Proverbs 16:25 —There is a way which seems right to a man, But its end is the way of death.

> Isaiah 53:6 —All of us like sheep have gone astray, each of us has turned to his own way; but the Lord has caused the iniquity of us all to fall on Him.

BECOMING LIKE OUR HUMBLE KING

Can you think of some Scriptures that confirm the folly of following your foolish pride and living life your own way? As I reflect on my walk with the Lord many times I let my own will take over, thinking in my heart: "Nobody is going to tell me what to do. I absolutely know what is best and I either do it my way, or I quit." When I succumb to this thinking, I am giving Satan a foothold in my heart and mind. I end up serving Satan's purposes and not the Lord's will. This fruit of pride dishonors the King of kings and bears rotten produce. As followers of the humble King we are exhorted in 1 Peter 5:6-8:

> Humble yourselves, therefore, under the mighty hand of God, that He may exalt you at the proper time, casting all your anxiety upon Him, because He cares for you. Be of sober spirit, be on the alert. Your adversary, the devil, prowls about like a roaring lion, seeking someone to devour.

It is important to understand how we are to humble ourselves. The Scriptures tell us to put ourselves under the mighty hand of God, the protection of the Lord, in order that in God's time He will lift you up. We need to continually throw all our cares, all our worries upon the Lord because He loves us and wants only the best for us.

Instead of being in a drunken, careless condition we are to be sober and watchful as we understand that the enemy of our souls wants to demolish our testimony and steal any fruit that would honor the Lord. We honor the Humble King by displaying the fruit of humility.

THE SIN OF INJUSTICE

The final *oy* mentioned has to do with injustice or unrighteousness.

> Isaiah 5:22-24 —Woe to those who are heroes in drinking wine, and valiant men in mixing strong drink; who justify the wicked for a bribe, and take away the rights of the ones who are in the right! Therefore, as a tongue of fire consumes stubble, and dry grass collapses into the flame, so their root will become like rot and their blossom blow away as dust; for they have rejected the law of the LORD of hosts, and despised the word of the Holy One of Israel.

In this section of Isaiah the Israelites were supposed to be enforcing the laws that would defend and protect those who had been defrauded, those who could not defend themselves. However, this was not the case as these men were military heroes and champions not only on the battlefield, but also in the drinking arena. Courage and honor did not mean anything to these so-called leaders, they could be bribed and the verdict given to the highest bidder.

The synonyms for injustice are qualities such as: unfairness, prejudice, inequality, bias, wrong, and discrimination. These actions of injustice follow the prideful men who see themselves as replacing the Lord's righteousness with their own perverted sense of justice. They are not producing the fruit of righteousness and justice that would reflect "The LORD —Our Righteousness."

> Jeremiah 23:6 —In His days Judah will be saved, and Israel will dwell securely; and this is His name by which He will be called, "The LORD our righteousness."

This rotten fruit of Israel failed in every aspect to reflect upon the character of our God. The question that God asks of Israel is what more could I have done for you? In other words, God has done everything for His vineyard, therefore what more could His vineyard possibly need or expect Him to do? Can you hear the pleading of God's heart through Isaiah as he sings this song?

His vineyard was planted in the richest soil where the Vinedresser Himself removed the rocky stones that could hinder growth. The soil was in the perfect location, a strong hill, where the vine would receive the needed sun for growth as well as be protected from the predators that would seek to destroy it. Everything was prepared with tender care as Israel's Beloved waited for His vine to produce good grapes.

WE HAVE EVERYTHING WE NEED

What has the Lord provided for you so that you might bear good fruit for your Beloved? Let's consider all that the Lord has done for us and praise Him along with King David,

Psalm 103: 1-2 —Bless the LORD, O my soul; And all that is within me, bless His holy name. Bless the LORD, O my soul, and forget none of His benefits.

Indeed what more could God do for us? Our Heavenly Vinedresser has planted us in the soil of His rich provisions and promises. Together let us grow in our appreciation and application of how we can bear fruit that will bring honor and glory to the Lord.

In the next chapter we take a deeper look as to why Israel did not bear good fruit. We are no different than the children of Israel in the day of Isaiah. We are involved in spiritual warfare and we need to know how to win this war.

THOUGHT QUESTIONS AND REFLECTIONS:

1. Think of creative ways you can communicate to your family and friends the truth of what God is doing in your life.

2. Pray about identifying and allowing God to remove the stones in your life that might be hindering your growth.

3. Read Psalm 103 reflecting on and giving thanks for all that the Lord has provided for you as his beloved daughter.

4. Pray about any small foxes that might be destroying your vineyard and ask the Lord to show you areas that you may have overlooked.

For though we walk in the flesh, we do not war
according to the flesh, for the weapons of our
warfare are not of the flesh, but divinely powerful
for the destruction of fortresses. We are destroying
speculations and every lofty thing rose up against
the knowledge of God, and we are taking every
thought captive to the obedience of Messiah.
2 Corinthians 10:3-5

Chapter 2

Spiritual Warfare

The Enemy Within

The 1980 comedy film *Private Benjamin* starring Goldie Hawn tells the story of Judy, a wealthy woman who joins the army when her husband dies on their wedding night. At first, Judy thinks the army will be like a structured country club, where she will forget all her troubles.

However, she quickly discovers that she has grossly misjudged the situation. Judy didn't understand that her basic training was to prepare her for the battles of war. Surprisingly after a series of mishaps and a rough start as an unfit recruit, she becomes a top notch soldier with confidence and good judgment to fight in the battles.

When I think about being in a spiritual war, I feel a little like Judy in *Private Benjamin*, thinking: "Is this what I signed up for when I became a believer in Messiah?

No one said anything about a war! Where is that abundant life I was promised?"

It is true, when we accept Yeshua as our Messiah, we are totally forgiven and fully accepted in the Beloved. Furthermore, Messiah told His disciples that, He was preparing a place for them in heaven, and not just for them but for all who loved His appearing. In light of that we desire to live with eternity in view. Nonetheless, there are great obstacles that keep us from this worthy and godly ambition. We might feel like Judy, not ready for any battles, but once we learn how to successfully wage the spiritual war, we will enjoy the fruit of the victory. The moment we become part of God's family, we are involved in spiritual warfare. Scripture informs us that living a godly life is a struggle. Paul, understanding the urgency of this matter, wrote to the believers in Corinth,

> 2 Corinthians 10:3-5 —For though we walk in the flesh, we do not war according to the flesh, for the weapons of our warfare are not of the flesh, but divinely powerful for the destruction of fortresses. We are destroying speculations and every lofty thing rose up against the knowledge of God, and we are taking every thought captive to the obedience of Messiah.

FIGHTING ON TWO FRONTS

Due to the fall of Satan, we have an adversary who wages war against God and all who belong to Him. Additionally, due to Adam's sin, we inherited sin nature, called flesh. When we put our trust in Messiah and His atoning sacrifice, we were transferred from darkness into the Kingdom of His Beloved Son, becoming a part of God's household. Therefore, it should come as no surprise that as the subjects of the King of kings we find ourselves engaged in a battle, and more than that, we are also fighting this war on two fronts. This war is both external and internal. In this external war we have two enemies: Satan and the world system. On the internal front is our flesh. It might seem overwhelming to us to realize the complexity of this battle. However, the truth is that neither Satan nor the world has the power to force any of us to go against God. It is our internal adversary that provides our external foes an opportunity to operate in our lives.

THE DOUBLE AGENT

The enemy within is called sin nature, or the flesh. In the Scriptures the sin nature and the flesh are used interchangeably and synonymously (Romans 7:18).

The flesh encompasses our body, soul and spirit. It is our carnality that gives both this world and the god of this age a foothold of power and influence in our lives. Our flesh is not our ally; our flesh does not have our best interest at heart, instead our flesh wants to destroy us. Giving into my flesh or self-will is the first front in this battle and is the primary reason I find myself acting in a rebellious and self-serving manner.

We might compare our flesh or sin nature to a double agent. In the book entitled, *What the Bible Teaches About Spiritual Warfare* by Robert Dean Jr. and Thomas Ice, they state that in the Scripture the flesh is mentioned fifty times as the primary enemy of the believer as opposed to only ten times, where demons or evil spirits are mentioned.

We may conclude that it is in our power to choose to yield to the Holy Spirit, or to give in to the desires of our flesh.

AN OFFERING THAT PLEASES GOD

In Genesis, the book of beginnings, we find an illustration that shows a distinction between the offering by flesh and the offering by faith.

> Genesis 4: 3-7 —So it came about in the course of time that Cain brought an offering to the LORD of the fruit of the ground. And Abel, on his part also brought of the firstlings of his flock and of their fat portions. And the LORD had regard for Abel and for his offering; but for Cain and for his offering He had no regard. So Cain became very angry and his countenance fell. Then the LORD said to Cain, "Why are you angry? And why has your countenance fallen? "If you do well, will not your countenance be lifted up? And if you do not do well, sin is crouching at the door; and its desire is for you, but you must master it."

What was the difference between Cain and Abel's sacrifices? Why was one accepted, but the other rejected by the Lord? The verse states that "the Lord had regard for Abel and for his offering," the word regard is *shaah* in Hebrew, and it means to gaze with interest or with favor. Why did Abel find favor in the sight of God? We find the answer to this question in Hebrews 11:4:

> By faith Abel offered to God a better sacrifice than Cain, through which he obtained the testimony that he was righteous, God testifying about his gifts, and through faith, though he is dead, he still speaks.

The reason why God was pleased with both Able and his offering was because he was offering his lamb by faith, and not in a fleshly attitude. In fact, Scripture teaches that it is impossible to please the Lord without faith, regardless of the size of the sacrifice (Hebrews 11:6).

Abel was a first example of faith. Like Abraham, Abel believed in the Lord; and He reckoned it to him as righteousness (Genesis 15:6). Abel by his faith offering was acknowledging that God was the provider of all and the source of his righteousness and success.

The fact that Abel offered the firstborn of his flock gives us further insight into Abel's faith and his worship. The word firstborn or firstfruits in Hebrew is *bikkurim*.

Leviticus 23 presents God's appointed times for Israel to meet with Him. One of His holy days is the celebration of the Firstfruits or *Yom Habikkurim* in Hebrew, which takes place fifty days after Passover. One of the significant points of this holiday has to do with presenting the firstfruits of their crops to the Lord, in order that the rest of the harvest would be accepted. Abel's offering to God was a forerunner of the celebration of firstfruits as he offered his first and the best to the Lord.

AN OFFERING THAT PLEASES THE FLESH

Cain, Abel's brother, gives us a negative example. The sacrifice offered according to the flesh will be rejected by God. In Genesis 4:5 we read, "But for Cain and for his offering He [God] had no regard." Cain found no favor in the eyes of God.

In Genesis 4:6 we read, "Then the Lord said to Cain, 'Why are you angry? And why has your countenance

fallen?'" The word countenance is *panim* in Hebrew and it simply means face. Cain's face reflected what was in his heart.

> Proverbs 27:19 —As in water face reflects face, so the heart of man reflects man.

He had a long sad face; Cain was sulking because he was angry with God. Therefore the Lord gives Cain some advice, "If you do well will not your countenance be lifted up?"

In Hebrew the phrase to do well is one word, *yatav*, which means to please God, and not oneself. Cain's offering was not to please God, but rather himself. God being gracious in His nature, continued to reach out to Cain.

> Genesis 4:7 —And if you do not do well [do not please me] then sin is crouching at the door; and its desire is for you, but you must master it.

The word desire in the Hebrew is *tesukah* and means longing to control. God wanted Cain to see his anger, his selfishness, and his desire to present an offering his way. When we seek to please God with our lives, we have to do it according to God's terms. The best way to honor God is through our obedience to His Word in humility.

The Lord gave Cain the solution. If you only seek to please Me and not yourself then this sin that is crouching at the door, will not master you. The solution was mastery of the sin nature through reliance upon the grace provided by God. Like Cain, we might want to please ourselves and have it our way. When God speaks, we better listen and heed the voice of the Lord. Cain is an example of walking in the flesh, and living life his own way.

Romans 14:23b gives us a definition of sin: "Whatever is not from faith is sin," meaning that any thought, word, or deed, no matter how noble, helpful, or religious, if it is not done in dependence upon God by walking in the Spirit, it is done in dependence upon our own powers, and God calls that sin.

PAUL UNDERSTOOD HIS FLESH

The sin nature also produces works that often are thought of as good. In Paul's case he was a respected scholar of the first rank and was considered a righteous man by his community.

However, after Paul met Yeshua on the road to Damascus, he understood what was worth living and dying for. What he once considered of great worth according to his flesh, now he will not glory in it, but rather count as worthless.

Our flesh naturally craves self-indulgence, reputation, and fame. But after meeting Messiah, his priorities permanently changed. There is nothing that this world can offer that would amount to knowing Yeshua. Here is Paul in his own words:

Philippians 3:3-9 —For we are the true circumcision, who worship in the Spirit of God and glory in Messiah Yeshua and put no confidence in the flesh, although I myself might have confidence even in the flesh. If anyone else has a mind to put confidence in the flesh, I far more: circumcised the eighth day, of the nation of Israel, of the tribe of Benjamin, a Hebrew of Hebrews; as to the Law, a Pharisee; as to zeal, a persecutor of

the church; as to the righteousness which is in the Law, found blameless. But whatever things were gain to me, those things I have counted as loss for the sake of Messiah. More than that, I count all things to be loss in view of the surpassing value of knowing Messiah Yeshua my Lord, for whom I have suffered the loss of all things, and count them but rubbish in order that I may gain Messiah, and may be found in Him, not having a righteousness of my own derived from the Law, but that which is through faith in Messiah, the righteousness which comes from God on the basis of faith.

However, it does not mean that it was easy for Paul to walk according to the Spirit. He shared the same struggle that each of us face. He can truly relate to the cycle of wanting to do good, avoid doing bad, and he understands the desperation of ongoing spiritual warfare from within. He described his own intense battle with the flesh:

Romans 7:18-25 —For I know that nothing good dwells in me, that is, in my flesh; for the wishing is present in me, but the doing of the good is not. For the good that I wish, I do not do; but I practice the very evil that I do not wish. But if I am doing the very thing I do not wish, I am no longer the one doing it, but sin which dwells in me. I find then the principle that evil is present in me, the one who wishes to do good. For I joyfully concur with the law of God in the inner man, but I see a different law in the members of my body, waging war against the law of my mind, and making me a prisoner of the law of sin which is in my members. Wretched man that I am! Who will set me free from the body of this death? Thanks be to God through Yeshua Messiah our Lord! So then, on the one hand I myself with my mind am serving the law of God, but on the other, with my flesh the law of sin.

DIVINELY POWERFUL WEAPONS

God is faithful and provides the way of escape. We have the Spirit of God indwelled in us. We have everything we need to live victoriously. God fights on our behalf, for we cannot win spiritual war by physical ammunitions, instead we win the spiritual war by divine weapons, by the armor that He alone provides.

Have you ever heard the phrase, Dress for success? Paul concludes his letter to the congregation at Ephesus by telling them how to dress for success against the enemies of God.

> Ephesians 6:10-12 —Finally, be strong in the Lord, and in the strength of His might. Put on the full armor of God, that you may be able to stand firm against the schemes of the devil. For our struggle is not against flesh and blood, but against the rulers, against the powers, against the world forces of this darkness, against the spiritual forces of wickedness in the heavenly places.

When I read, "put on the full armor of God" I think of the knights in ancient history clad with their clunky metal armor from head to toe. This kind of protective covering does not appeal to me at all. In today's society women are welcome in the military. In Israel both men and women upon graduation from high school are expected to serve in the Israeli Defense Forces. As women serve in the military they need to clothe themselves with protective gear including helmets, bullet proof vests, combat boots, and other armor preparing them for battle. I am exhausted

just thinking about this armor not to mention the fact that all this battle regalia would probably make me look at least twenty pounds heavier. Thankfully, the armor of God is not physical, but spiritual; it is not visible, but invisible; therefore it will not add any physical weight, but rather will provide protection from the inside out.

DRESS RIGHT FOR THE OCCASION

The section begins with the words, "Be strong in the Lord, and in the strength of His might" and this is the key to success. Warning! Do not ever try to fight this war in your own puny strength, but be diligent to depend fully upon the Lord. One of the names for God is *Adonai -Tzva'ot*, which means the Lord of Armies.

We could never fight this battle against the rulers, the powers, the world forces of darkness, and the spiritual forces of wickedness without the Lord of Hosts as our Commander-in- Chief. He is the one we look to for victory and it is only in His strength that we can stand firm against all enemies. But what does it mean to put on the armor of God? One of my favorite verses about what to wear is found in the closet of Isaiah:

> Isaiah 61:10 —I will rejoice greatly in the LORD, My soul will exult in my God; for He has clothed me with garments of salvation, He has wrapped me with a robe of righteousness, As a bridegroom decks himself with a garland, and as a bride adorns herself with her jewels.

The expression "clothed me" in Hebrew is similar to the Greek expression to put on and carries the idea of permanence. This clothing and equipment for defense is not something you remove when you take a shower and retire for the evening, it is designed especially for you, and it comes with lifetime warranty. Paul exhorts the believers in Rome to live for the Lord and to put on their armor while there is still time:

> Romans 13:12-14 —The night is almost gone, and the day is at hand. Let us therefore lay aside the deeds of darkness and put on the armor of light. Let us behave properly as in the day, not in carousing and drunkenness, not in sexual promiscuity and sensuality, not in strife and jealousy. But put on the Lord Yeshua the Messiah, and make no provision for the flesh in regard to its lusts.

Note that Paul uses the phrase put on two times in these verses. First, he encourages them to clothe themselves in the armor of light then to put on the Messiah Himself. As we take a closer look at the armor that is listed in Ephesians 6:10-18, we must realize that this protective covering reflects the very character of Yeshua the Messiah.

FREE TO WALK IN THE TRUTH

> Ephesians 6:14a —Stand firm therefore, having girded your loins with truth.

First we have the girdle of truth. I remember years ago I was trying to wear a girdle in order to make my stomach look flatter, but my good intentions quickly faded because the girdle was so uncomfortable that I had to run home and rip it off. Paul is taking a familiar idea from those in his culture, who wore flowing robes while in their homes. However during work or warfare these robes would be tied around the waist in order to free the individual to

labor or to fight. At the first Passover meal in Egypt the Israelites were told to eat with their loins girded (Exodus 12:11). Their clothing was tied up around the waist; they had their sandals on their feet with staff in hand signifying they were ready to walk out the door whenever God told them it was time to leave.

But what does a belt of truth mean for us today? First of all, we must keep in mind that truth is the character of God as revealed in Messiah (John 14:6). Therefore, when we surround ourselves with the truth of God we can defeat the father of lies (John 8:44). What a beautiful way to describe our weapons of warfare as Paul tells the congregation at Ephesus to clothe themselves in the armor of light (Romans 13:12). Think of the girdle of truth, surrounding your life with His light, His clarity. The light of God always dispels the darkness of Satan; we will have victory when we let His truth lift the clothing or whatever is preventing us from walking in His light.

WE ARE HIS TAPESTRY

I am often amazed with the beautiful needlework my friends can create. The tapestry looks so perfect from the top, but if you turn over this same tapestry, you will see dangling threads, messy spots and uneven areas. As God observes our lives, He sees us as His beautiful handiwork that He created for His good works. He desires to shine His light into every area of our hearts and souls. When I think of this belt of truth I can see the Lord giving me His heavenly viewpoint and shedding His light on my path as He takes care of all the loose ends, the messy spots, the seemingly unfinished areas. Like those Israelites at the first Passover we need to be ready to follow whenever and wherever the Lord leads us to go as He shows us His way.

PROTECTION FOR THE HEART AND EMOTIONS

Ephesians 6:14b —And having put on the breastplate of righteousness

The breastplate of righteousness is the next piece of Spiritual formfitting garment. Since one of the names for the Lord is *Jehovah Tzidkenu* - The Lord is our Righteousness, we can quickly see how this breastplate reflects the character of God.

The very righteousness of God was ascribed to us when we trusted in Messiah's atonement for our sins. So this righteous protective clothing that covers our vital organs positions us to not only stand in the righteousness of Messiah, but also gives us the ability to live out God's true standard in this world.

Today the injustice of our society can be overwhelming, nevertheless, His righteousness guards us. He is the only one who is always right and embodies what true justice is. When we falter and do not know what is right or true, we just need to recognize that we are protected by His justice, and His fairness.

Paul refused to identify with the righteousness of his own derived from the Law, but instead relied on the righteousness that is attained through faith in Messiah. Jeremiah prophesied about the day that the Lord will be our Righteousness (Jeremiah 23:6). We are only truly dressed when we are covered with His righteousness, which comes from God on the basis of faith. When we are dressed

in His Righteousness we can withstand the attacks of guilt and condemnation. Romans 8:1 assures us that there is no condemnation for those who are in Messiah Yeshua.

THE GOOD NEWS OF SHALOM SHOES

Ephesians 6:15 —And having shod your feet with the preparation of the gospel of peace

Shoes are very important when going to war. In fact, the boots that the Roman soldiers wore had special hobnails in the soles to give them better footing during the battles. These shoes enabled the soldier to stand firm against the enemy. I am not interested in hobnailed boots, but for some of us shoes can be a wardrobe obsession.

On a recent TV talk show one young woman confessed to buying over 200 pairs of shoes with her credit card. Her myriad of shoes were lined up before her on the stage and she admitted on national TV that she needed help. Maybe you don't share such an addiction to shopping, but many of us can identify with this woman, who was trying desperately to fill the emptiness in her life.

A hollowness that neither her good job nor her cute fiancé could fill. I wanted to reach through the TV and tell her that she needs only one pair of shoes to find the peace that she longs for, that the only way to find peace with God and herself is to accept Messiah's peace. And when she discovers *shalom* (peace) with God through Messiah's atonement she will understand that she is complete in Him (Colossians 2:10). She will appreciate that her Beloved desires her to return and be reconciled to Him and understand that "having been justified by faith, we have peace with God through our Lord Yeshua the Messiah" (Romans 5:1).

What wonderful shoes the Lord gives us to wear. Not only will they never wear out but we can also have beautiful feet as we are sent out in our Good News of shalom shoes. We can be heralds of this life-giving message the world needs to hear.

> Isaiah 52:7 —How lovely on the mountains are the feet of him who brings good news, who announces peace And brings good news of happiness, who announces salvation, and says to Zion, "Your God reigns!"

DEFENSIVE WEAPONS- THE SHIELD OF FAITH

> Ephesians 6:16 —In addition to all, taking up the shield of faith with which you will be able to extinguish all the flaming missiles of the evil one.

We have just discussed our offensive weapons of warfare, the girdle of truth, the breastplate of righteousness and the *Shalom Shoes* which are to be worn at all times. The final three pieces of armor are weapons of defense to take up in the heat of battle.

Utilizing the shield of faith is the only way to extinguish Satan's fiery missiles. This faith is living faith that trusts in the promises and power of our covenant-keeping God. We must put our confidence in the Lord and not rely upon our own works. The Scriptures are clear,

> Proverbs 30:5-6 —Every word of God is tested; He is a shield to those who take refuge in Him. Do not add to His words lest He reprove you, and you be proved a liar.

Think of it this way: if you are trusting God when the enemy attacks your shield will deflect those flaming darts of Satan which could come in the form of lies, discouragement, doubt, your self-sufficiency, false teachers and persecution. Our security continues as we depend upon our mighty God.

DON'T FORGET TO PUT YOUR HAT ON!

Ephesians 6:17a —And take the helmet of salvation, and the sword of the Spirit, which is the word of God

The next defensive weapon is called a helmet of salvation. When my sons were young and it was one of those frigid New York winter days I would say to them, "Don't go outside without putting your hats on." Just as those hats protected my sons from the harsh winter cold so, too, we need this offensive head covering to protect our minds. The helmet of salvation refers to a mind that is controlled by God.

There are three aspects of salvation, which includes the past, the present, and the future. As a junior in high school I accepted Yeshua as my Savior. At that point I was saved from the penalty of sin (Galatians 2:20). Over these many years I have grown in the Lord and I can affirm that growing in my salvation means freedom from the devastating power of sin (Romans 6:11-14). But wait! The best is yet to come. I am looking forward to that day when I will be with my Beloved, the King of kings, where I will be eternally free from the presence of sin (Romans 8:18).

We should be filling our minds with the fact that we are justified before the Lord, and as we confess daily our sins, we are cleansed and sanctified then finally we will be glorified for eternity. These truths will keep our thoughts and minds secure in Him.

THE MORE YOU USE IT THE SHARPER IT GETS

During his college years, my son Josh sold *Cutco* knives as a part-time job. It was a short lived enterprise but I did buy a set of these very sharp knives. It turns out that my old knives were dull compared to the new knives and it was many cut fingers later that I finally learned how to respect and use these sharp instruments.

The Scriptures compare the Word of God to be even sharper than any two-edged sword.

> Hebrews 4:12-13 —For the word of God is living and active and sharper than any two-edged sword, and piercing as far as the division of soul and spirit, of both joints and marrow, and able to judge the thoughts and intentions of the heart. And there is no creature hidden from His sight, but all things are open and laid bare to the eyes of Him with whom we have to do.

We need to respect and learn to utilize this offensive weapon, and keep in mind that the Sword of the Spirit gets sharper with use. Messiah, who is our example, demonstrated His skillful use of the Word of God. When He was tempted by Satan in the wilderness, he restrained Himself from using His miraculous power, but rather replied to each temptation with the words, "It is written." Yeshua refuted Satan's lies with the absolute truth of God's Word, thereby defeating the enemy. It is vital to be a student of the Word, otherwise we become an easy target for the false accusations and lies of our adversary.

We must see the study of the Word as essential, in order to help us handle our sharp sword and wield it correctly against all kinds of assaults. We need to spend time studying and encouraging each other in the truths of God's Word.

PRAY ALWAYS FOR EVERYONE

Prayer is mentioned as the final weapon in our arsenal. This mighty weapon can be used anytime and anywhere. In fact, prayer is always our first line of defense and our greatest resource. Through prayer we are putting on our protective clothing, and through praise and thanksgiving we enter His presence.

> Psalms 100:4 —Enter into his gates with thanksgiving, and into his courts with praise: be thankful unto him, and bless his name.

We are commanded to "rejoice always; pray without ceasing; in everything give thanks; for this is God's will for you in Messiah Yeshua" (1 Thessalonians 5:16-18).

Paul concludes this section by exhorting the believers at Ephesus and us to be praying always in the power of the Holy Spirit reminding us to stay alert and persist in our prayers for fellow believers.

> Ephesians 6:18-19 —With all prayer and petition pray at all times in the Spirit, and with this in view, be on the alert with all perseverance and petition for all the saints and pray on my behalf, that utterance may be given to me in the opening of my mouth, to make known with boldness the mystery of the gospel.

We have quite an arsenal to carry on in this victorious

warfare. Let's review your radiant and airy armor of light that you should wear for every occasion. You can dress for success with:

- ❧ Your belt of truth that surrounds you
- ❧ Your breastplate of righteousness that covers your heart
- ❧ Your formfitting shalom shoes
- ❧ Your shield of faith
- ❧ Your head covered with His salvation
- ❧ The Eternal Word of God

And in conclusion, don't forget to keep praying!

THOUGHT QUESTIONS AND REFLECTIONS:

1. Discuss the two battle fronts in our spiritual warfare.

2. When you consider Cain and Abel and their offerings, who do you identify with in attitude and actions?

3. How did Paul understand his flesh and what does this teach us about ourselves?

4. Review the various weapons that we have as believers and consider any weak areas you may have.

5. Ask yourself the question, "Am I dressed for success today?"

Every branch of mine that does not bear fruit
He takes away, and every branch that does bear
fruit he prunes, that it may bear more fruit.

John 15:2

Chapter 3

Abiding in the Beloved

Bearing Much Fruit

I love all kinds of fruit, but my ideal fruit is a perfectly ripe kiwi. Even though the kiwi does not look like much on the outside, it is quite tasty and sweet inside. Even the kiwi's warm and inviting green color is attractive to me. Whenever I find a bowl of mixed fruit where kiwis are added, I try to load my plate with all the green circles I can manage.

On the other hand, a bad kiwi tastes terrible. If it's too mushy and overripe, watch out! If it's too hard, it is impossible to enjoy. A kiwi, just like any other fruit, needs to be the precise ripeness in order to taste the way it was meant to taste. Then and only then, it can be fully enjoyed.

Our lives are always producing fruit. In light of this, the question can be raised, "What kind of fruit will delight God's heart? I believe that what we think and know about God will reflect the fruit our lives produce. Since we are created in God's image, we possess the potential of reflecting His character and thus bringing glory to His Name. But in order for our lives to emanate His sweet fruit of righteousness to the fullest, we must have an intimate relationship with Yeshua. As Paul tells the congregation in Philippi, "having been filled with the fruit of righteousness which comes through Yeshua the Messiah, to the glory and praise of God" (Philippians 1:11).

In Isaiah 5, we studied the song of Isaiah's Beloved. Israel was planted as God's vineyard and although Israel's Beloved did everything so that the vine would produce good fruit, only rotten fruit appeared. We noted that the vineyard was a picture of the spiritual life of Israel and the fruit that God was expecting Israel to make would be spiritual fruit.

In John 15 Messiah Yeshua is speaking about a vineyard and bearing fruit as well. In context, He is encouraging His disciples, in light of the fact that He will be offering Himself up as the Passover Lamb and will be giving His life the next day.

When Messiah begins to talk about the Vine and the branches, He is using symbols the disciples are very familiar with. In Jewish homes every Shabbat, the evening begins with a special blessing that is recited over the fruit of the vine. And during the Passover meal this same prayer is recited four times when the cups of wine are drunk.

THE CUP OF REDEMPTION

Luke 22:20 —And in the same way He took the cup after they had eaten, saying, "This cup which is poured out for you is the new covenant in My blood."

Around the Passover table while the disciples were considering the deep red color of the wine and remembering the blood of the Lamb, suddenly Messiah gives new significance to this cup of wine.

Yeshua establishes the New Covenant, fulfilling the prophecy found in Jeremiah 31: 31-34. Messiah was about to leave His disciples and He guarantees them in various ways that this is the beginning of a deeper, more intimate relationship as He promises to send His disciples the Holy Spirit.

John 14:26 — But the Helper, the Holy Spirit, whom the Father will send in My name, He will teach you all things, and bring to your remembrance all that I said to you.

Messiah is reminding His disciples that He is doing the will of the Father because of His love for the Father (John 14:31). In Philippians 2:8b we read, "He humbled Himself by becoming obedient to the point of death, even death on a cross." Messiah is teaching His disciples that His obedience is proof of His love for His Father.

YOU ARE NEVER ALONE

During this special celebration of Passover, Messiah gave them words of truth and encouragement. In preceding chapters Yeshua told them that He will be leaving them, in order to prepare a place for them. However, He will not leave them alone, His presence will continue to be with them through the ministry of the Holy Spirit, who would be their comforter and supplier of every need.

In John 15, Messiah begins to reinforce His teaching with vivid poetic symbols of the vine and the vinedresser. We also learn what Messiah expects from His disciples while He is away. Yeshua is now directing their attention to certain great truths, which He wants them to grasp and remember while He is gone. Messiah begins by urging them to understand the absolute necessity of the close union and communion they each need to have with Him and one another.

THE VINE AND THE VINEDRESSER

John 15:1 —I am the true vine, and my Father is the vinedresser.

What an interesting way to introduce Himself. Yeshua knew that his disciples were familiar with vineyards and the fruit of the vine since it was such a vital part of daily life in Israel. We see Him taking the ordinary and giving extraordinary meaning to it.

When Yeshua says, "I am the true vine," He refers to the fact that He is the true, original vine of which all other vines are only types and shadows. Similarly, Messiah is the true Bread of heaven as opposed to the manna in the wilderness. He is also the true Light of the world and John the baptizer was a lamp to point to the true eternal Light.

Israel also is referred to as the vine that was supposed to produce good fruit and point all nations of the world to the

Beloved. In Isaiah chapter 5 we learned that Israel failed miserably in their spiritual service to God.

However, now everything is different because Messiah has come. Yeshua declares that He is the true Vine and His Father is the Vinedresser. The word "fruit" is repeated eight times in John 15 and signifies that this chapter is not about salvation, but rather about fruit bearing and being productive.

The book *The Disciplemaker* by Gary Derickson and Earl Radmacher, sheds light on what it means for God the Father to take on this position as the vinedresser.

> A vinedresser is more than a mere farmer. His work is not like the typical farmer who simply plows up a field, plants a crop, harvests it and waits for the next season. Grapes are more than an annual crop. They are individuals. A husbandman must know all about the grapes, how they grow, what they need, when they need it and what produces the best health as well as production in the plant. But to be effective, they not only must know the right things, but they must nurture their plants with loving care.
>
> The vinedresser's grape vines remain with him for decades. He comes to know each one in a personal way, much like a shepherd with his sheep. He knows how the vine is faring from year to year and which ones are more productive or vigorous than others. He knows what they respond to and what special care certain one's need. Every vine has its own personality. And the vinedresser comes to know it over the years. The vinedresser cares for each vine and nurtures it, pruning it the appropriate amount at the appropriate times, fertilizing it, lifting its branches from the ground and propping them or tying them to the trellis, and taking measure to protect them from insects and disease.

Today our vineyards have grown in size and our individual notice and attention has probably been lost in most cases. But in ancient times the vineyards were smaller and so each vine could be known by the vinedresser. When God Himself is our Vinedresser, we the branches can experience complete confidence and security.

HOW TO PRODUCE REALLY GOOD FRUIT

John 15:2, 5 —Every branch of mine that does not bear fruit he takes away, and every branch that does bear fruit he prunes, that it may bear more fruit. I am the vine, you are the branches; he who abides in Me, and I in him, he bears much fruit; for apart from Me you can do nothing.

As the true Vine, Messiah demonstrates to His followers, the branches, how bearing fruit actually works. The question may arise: "But is it not enough to be a branch of the Vine and be attached to Him?" I believe that this section in John shows that if we truly are attached and part of the Vine then the purpose of this relationship will be seen in the fruit that comes forth as we obey the Lord. The fruit is the proof that we are truly in relationship, the evidence that we are children of the Lord. This spiritual fruit that we are to produce represents God's likeness, His character lived out in us. In these verses we are not looking at the fruit itself, but how this fruit is to be produced.

When Messiah begins His teaching by stating, "I am the true vine and My Father is the Vinedresser," He is reminding His disciples that a vine needs a vinedresser or husbandman to watch over it. The vine is dependent on the vinedresser to plant, prune, water, and protect it. Here Messiah is showing the relationship that He had been living out before His disciples during His earthly ministry. Yeshua just taught them about His relationship with His Father. From John 14:10 He says,

> Do you not believe that I am in the Father, and the Father is in Me? The words that I say to you I do not speak on My own initiative, but the Father abiding in Me does His works.

Note that Messiah is already abiding in the Father and the Father in Him. It was out of this dependent relationship that Yeshua confidently entered death and the grave assured that His Father would raise Him up. All that Messiah was and all that Messiah did, was a direct result of His dependence on the Father. Think about their relationship. Messiah said, "I and the Father are One" (John 10:30). Can they get any closer? From His example we learn that Messiah was totally dependent on the Father and this confidence led Him to give Himself as the Lamb of God.

In light of His example how much more do we need to understand and acknowledge our dependence on the Vine who is depending on the Vinedresser.

I believe that we as women desire and long for intimacy. This intimacy and closeness is there for us and can be found in our dependent relationship with our Beloved, the Vine. And as a result of this primary relationship with our Beloved we can then be enabled to be open and intimate with our husbands and friends.

LIFTING UP THE VINES

John 15:2 —Every branch of mine that does not bear fruit He *takes away*, and every branch that does bear fruit he prunes, that it may bear more fruit.

The phrase "takes away" is from the Greek word, *airo*, and the primary meaning is to raise, to lift, to take up, or pick up. From the word *airo* we get the words airplane and aerodynamics.

How does the Vinedresser lift the branch or raise up the branch? In Israel the branches of the grapevines are often laying on the ground during the dormant season. However, when the fruit-bearing season arrives the vinedresser begins to lift the branches off the ground in order for the sun to envelop the branch. As the sun envelops all sides of the branch the fruit can ripen to its full potential. If this is not done then the branch is left on the ground and will begin to sink its roots in the shallow surface of the surrounding soil where the branch cannot receive enough moisture to bring forth anything but stinking, hard, little grapes.

In the lifting process the branches are forced to derive their nutrients from the deep roots of the vine. The branches are also exposed to the sun that will cause them to flourish. How encouraging to think that Messiah does not condemn us for being fruitless, but rather desires to lift, cleanse and shine His healing light on us so we can produce good fruit.

According to John 15:2, "Every branch that does bear fruit He prunes, that it may bear more fruit," what does the Vinedresser do to a vine that does bear fruit? The word prune is *kathairo* in Greek and means to cleanse of filth and impurity. It also carries the idea of expiation from guilt.

As Messiah was speaking to His disciples, I wonder if he was thinking of Peter and how his life would unfold in the next few days. When Peter was with Messiah, following close to Him, he made bold statements.

> John 13:36-38 —Simon Peter said to Him, "Lord, where are You going?" Yeshua answered, "Where I go, you cannot follow Me now; but you shall follow later." Peter said to Him, "Lord, why can I not follow You right now? I will lay down my life for You." Yeshua answered, "Will you lay down your life for Me? Truly, truly, I say to you, a cock shall not crow, until you deny Me three times.

LIFTING PETER UP

In this passage Messiah is teaching principles to His disciples that will lead them to His instruction on how to bear fruit, more fruit, and much fruit. In stark contrast, just several hours after this teaching takes place, Messiah was arrested.

Instead of staying close by, Peter followed from afar and did not identify with Messiah and His sufferings. He denied the Lord three times, each time becoming more emphatic (John 18:25-27). Did these actions finish Peter's relationship with His Master? Had he ruined his chances to be useful and produce fruit for the kingdom? Peter mistakenly warmed himself at the enemy's fire and let the shoots from his branch sink into the shallow soil of the world and its values for a brief time. It is recorded in Matthew 26:75 that as soon as Peter realized what he had done he went out and wept bitterly.

MESSIAH TO THE RESCUE

After Messiah's shameful crucifixion, Peter had suggested that they all go fishing. Perhaps he was looking to justify his existence and do something where he was proficient and could be fruitful. But after a night of fishing their nets were still empty (John 21:3).

How depressing and discouraging that must have been especially for Peter since it was his idea. We can almost feel how Peter's sense of failure was escalating. He not only failed to be faithful to His Master in His darkest moment, a time when Yeshua needed him the most, but even now, Peter is failing at something that was his field of expertise, fishing.

They had not caught a single fish after fishing all night. Suddenly, when they least expected it, Messiah appeared and instructed them to cast their nets on the other side of the boat. After heeding to Yeshua's suggestion and not relying on their own experience, their nets were full of fish. Then John recognized that it was their Master, Yeshua, and he said to Peter, "It is the Lord" (John 21:7). Instead of sailing the boat back to the shore, Peter, being Peter, jumps out of the boat into the water and swims as fast as he can to embrace Yeshua.

A SPECIAL MEAL

Peter forgetting all his insecurities and being overwhelmed by seeing his beloved Master, rushes first to greet Him. Yeshua tells Peter to bring Him some of the fish that they caught because He understood the physical needs of Peter and His disciples, He knew that they must be hungry and tired after fishing all night. Then Messiah cooks breakfast for them. Yeshua waits until after they eat to speak to Peter. Like Peter, when I feel discouraged, disappointed, or depressed in order to lift my sagging esteem, and regain my dignity, I need to remember that Messiah understands my physical and emotional needs. And just as Peter did, I need to get out of my boat of failures and jump into the waters of His love, forgetting all my shortcomings and insecurities, running into the arms of my Beloved. Only then will my joy be restored.

PETER IS RESTORED

The Gospel accounts inform us that Messiah indeed lifted Peter out of his pit of remorse and guilt. In Yeshua's final resurrection appearance, before He ascended to heaven, He visited the disciples in Galilee.

John 21:15-19 —So when they had finished breakfast, Yeshua said to Simon Peter, "Simon, son of John, do you love (*agape*) Me more than these?" He said to Him, "Yes, Lord; You know that I love (*phileo*) You." He said to him, "Tend (feed) My lambs." He said to him again a second time, "Simon, son of John, do you love (agape) Me?" He said to Him, "Yes, Lord; You know that I love (*phileo*) You." He said to him, "Shepherd [like a Vinedresser] My sheep." He said to him the third time, "Simon, son of John, do you love (*phileo*) Me?" Peter was grieved because He said to him the third time, "Do you love (*phileo*) Me?" And he said to Him, "Lord, You know all things; You know that I love You." Yeshua said to him, "Tend My sheep. "Truly, truly, I say to you, when you were younger, you used to gird yourself, and walk wherever you wished; but when you grow old, you will stretch out your hands, and someone else will gird you, and bring you where you do not wish to go." Now this He said, signifying by what kind of death he would glorify God. And when He had spoken this, He said to him, "Follow Me!"

Yeshua initiates dialogue concerning the most sensitive issue for Peter. He knew that Peter needed to deal with the pain of remorse over rejecting Him. Peter also needed forgiveness and affirmation of Yeshua's love. Instead of confronting Peter, he gives him an opportunity to express his love and devotion.

The resurrected Messiah had already died for Peter's sin. The words of forgiveness and love were flowing from Messiah's lips; nonetheless, Peter desperately needed to be released from his sense of guilt in order to accept Messiah's love. Only then could Peter go and bear fruit for Messiah. Peter was in need of a lesson on knowing the depth of God's grace for himself before he could share it with others.

Yeshua gently asked Peter three times, "Do you love Me more than these?" Peter was challenged to think of bearing more fruit as he affirmed his love for Messiah. Peter knew that in order to live and to die for Him, he would have to abide in the Vine, for apart from Messiah he could do nothing.

AGAPE PLUS PHILEO EQUALS AHAVAH

There is a strong difference of opinion among noted Greek scholars about the interchanging of the English word "love" for both Greek words, *phileo* (brotherly love) and *agape* (God's love). I tend to agree with F. F. Bruce in his commentary on John:

When two distinguished Greek scholars, both arguing from the standards of classical Greek see the significance of the synonyms so differently, we may wonder if indeed we are intended to see such distinct significance. The facts are that in the Septuagint to render one and the same Hebrew word *ahavah*. In other words both Greek words are used interchangeably for the *ahavah*, love in Hebrew.

The point for us is this: Peter reaffirms his love for the Lord and Yeshua reaffirms His choice of him as an apostle, therefore entrusting Peter with the flock. Peter is commissioned by Messiah for service not only to be an evangelist, but also a shepherd. The fact that Messiah asked him the question, "Do you love me?" three times, may correlate with the fact that Peter had denied Yeshua three times. But could it also correlate with the idea that Messiah is calling Him to bear fruit, bear more fruit, and bear much fruit?

PETER'S CALLING AFFIRMED

God was not surprised by Peter's failures. In fact, He even publicly foretold Peter, "you will deny Me" (John 13:38). Most of us can identify with Peter. Even though he was quick to respond and was the most outspoken disciple, he had a passion to please the Lord. He desired to bring honor to the Lord with his life. In his moment of weakness, he gave into his flesh; consequently Peter denied Yeshua, bearing fruit of the flesh. And when Peter expected judgment, he received mercy. God did not put Peter down, but rather lifted him up, restored him and was able to use Peter to extend His Kingdom in mighty ways. Peter learned what it meant to abide in the Vine and then to bear fruit.

He was lifted (*airo*) and cleansed (*katharias*) by the words of Yeshua. He grew in his ability to bear fruit and had the privilege of laying down his own life for Messiah's sake. I think we could all agree that Peter first, bore fruit, then more fruit then much fruit!

When Yeshua asks us the question: "Do you love Me more than the people or things around you? What can we say? I desire like Peter to affirm, "Yes, Lord I love you and I am willing to serve you in whatever way you desire."

Our confidence is not in ourselves but in the Lord, who lifts us up, cleanses us, and nurtures us so we will bear fruit for Him.

We need to examine our lives to see if we are attached to the Vine or are we getting careless and letting our shoots go into shallow, vain activities. These activities may even look like fruit, but in the end they produce sour, hard, and uneatable little grapes.

A LESSON ON HUMILITY

John 13:12-17 —And so when He had washed their feet, and taken His garments, and reclined at the table again, He said to them, "Do you know what I have done to you? You call Me Teacher and Lord; and you are right, for so I am. If I then, the Lord and the Teacher, washed your feet, you also ought to wash one another's feet. For I gave you an example that you also should do as I did to you. Truly, truly, I say to you, a slave is not greater than his master; neither is one who is sent greater than the one who sent him. If you know these things, you are blessed if you do them."

The Passover Seder begins with the ceremonial cleansing of hands by the one, who has the honor of leading the Seder. Our Master used this ceremony to teach His followers a lesson on servant leadership. Messiah arose from the table and instead of taking the honor to wash His hands, He began to wash their feet. In giving them this example of humble service, He was expecting them to follow His pattern of humility.

Do you think that Peter easily forgot His Master washing His feet? As he was sinking to the lowest points of disobedience, He would remember Yeshua kneeling before him, pouring the water over his feet, and drying them. He would remember that His Lord cared enough about Him to teach him these eternal truths.

Conversely when Peter is used in mighty and awesome ways to bring honor to the Lord he could have become proud and arrogant. When Peter preached he saw 3000 come to faith at Shavuot (Acts 2:41). Peter would need to remember that he was a servant of Messiah and attached to the Vine realizing that this fruit was a direct result of him being attached to the Vine.

BEING PRUNED

John 15:3 —Already you are clean [pruned] because of the word that I have spoken to you.

In this section Yeshua teaches His disciples how to be cleansed. The word for clean or prune is based on the Greek word cleanse, *kathario.* The Hebrew equivalent to *kathario* is *tahor,* meaning clean and pure both physically and spiritually. To be spiritually pure (*tahor*) meant to be free from corrupt desire, sin, and guilt. When a priest (*cohen*) entered into his period of service in the temple, he began first by going through the process of becoming ceremonially clean himself before the Lord. First, he had to have a full bathing. This included special washings as well as offering certain sacrifices. When he had completed the cleansing process, he was qualified to serve intercede on behalf of others.

Since the disciples were already believers and were already forgiven, this pruning is not referring to cleansing from the penalty of sin, but rather has the idea of cleansing that would make them ready to bear fruit.

This is what Messiah is picturing here as He is speaking to His disciples. God through His Word can purge specific sins from someone's life. As the vine is cleansed by pruning, it is made clean and pure in order to bear fruit.

ABIDE IN ME AND I IN YOU

John 15:4-5 —Abide in Me, and I in you. As the branch cannot bear fruit of itself, unless it abides in the vine, so neither can you, unless you abide in Me. I am the vine, you are the branches; he who abides in Me, and I in him, he bears much fruit; for apart from Me you can do nothing.

Messiah goes on to teach Peter, and the rest of us, what is needed to be fruitful. Yeshua said, "Abide in Me, and I in you." What does it mean to abide? This Greek word for abide is *meno,* which means to remain, to stay, to live, and to continue. A vine branch is lifeless and useless unless it remains attached to the vine. The living sap from the stock flows into the branch, enabling it to produce grapes. Similarly in our lives, it is when we remain in union with Messiah and derive our life from Him, only then will we produce the fruit of the Spirit. Paul reiterates this truth in his epistles.

Galatians 2:20 —I have been crucified with Messiah. It is no longer I who live, but Messiah who lives in me. And the life I now live in the flesh I live by faith in the Son of God, who loved me and gave himself for me.

Philippians 4:13 —I can do all things through Him who strengthens me.

This calls us to vigilance because abiding is not a casual idea of let's hang out together, rather abiding means a sustained conscious communion with the Lord, whereby we maintain our fellowship with Him.

John 15:4 says, "Abide in me and I in you." The two things are distinct, though closely connected. "I in you" is a matter of grace and takes place when we trust in Messiah as our atonement.

The other phrase, "abide in me" refers to our responsibility to look to Him for all our resources, in order to see His goodness, His grace, and His power in every situation as He enables us to bear fruit.

The final phrase, "without Him we can do nothing" reinforces the fact that we are totally dependent on what He alone can provide. Most likely our pride will agree to assistance, but not surrender. However, it is our yielded hearts that the Lord is looking for and our acknowledgment of our total dependence on Him.

A SHAKY BRANCH

Peter, who may have started His ministry as a shaky branch, learned the secret of abiding. He knew that he was totally dependent on the Lord and likewise discipled others. He urges all of us to humble ourselves and depend on God to give us our dignity and significance. When we read Peter's epistles, we can notice his change in attitude that abiding in Messiah produced. His writing is permeated with gentleness, meekness, and humility. Peter grew from being a fisherman to a follower of Yeshua, to becoming His disciple, and finally being Messiah's friend (1 Peter 5:5-7).

BEARING FRUIT

Messiah is teaching His disciples how to bear fruit, bear more fruit, and bear much fruit. In John 15:5 Messiah repeats, "I am the vine, you are the branches; he who abides in Me, and I in him, he bears much fruit; for apart from Me you can do nothing." Messiah knowing of His impending death, wants to strengthen their faith. His earnest desire is that they keep abiding in Him.

It is important to remember that abiding is not automatic, but rather is a deliberate choice that His disciples will have to make daily. Messiah gives the contrast and lets them know that if they think they can do something apart from Him, they are sadly mistaken. However, He wants to assure them that they are eternally secure in His hand.

John 10:27-29 —My sheep hear My voice, and I know them, and they follow Me; and I give eternal life to them, and they shall never perish; and no one shall snatch them out of My hand. My Father, who has given them to Me, is greater than all; and no one is able to snatch them out of the Father's hand.

We are eternally secure in Him but in order to produce fruit we must abide. Messiah wants His sheep, as He calls us in John 10 and His branches as He calls us in John 15, to realize we have choices each day to abide, or not to abide.

John 15:6 —If anyone does not abide in Me, he is thrown (cast) away as a branch, and dries up; (shrivels up) and they (those who had been watching) gather them, and cast them into the fire, and they are burned.

The purpose of abiding is to bear fruit. I like the way the authors of *The DiscipleMaker* explained this verse:

Rather than being a warning of discipline or judgment, John 15:6 is an illustration of uselessness in light of post-harvest, dormancy inducing pruning. The best illustration of the uselessness resulting from a failure to abide with the vine-branch analogy could only come from the post harvest pruning. Everything purged in early Spring was either growing from a branch (sprigs and suckers), the branch not being removed, or from an undesired location on the trunk. Only at the end of the season would there be branches removed, piled up and burned.

In fact, Yeshua may have chosen to allude to post harvest cultural practices specifically because He did not want His disciples to mistakenly link fruitfulness to divine discipline. Rather, He wanted them to see the importance of abiding itself. In the vineyard, anything not attached to the vine is useless and discarded. A part of the discarding process at the end of the productive season is the burning of dry materials. The burning need not describe judgment, but is simply one of the steps in the process being described. It is simply what happens to pruned material. The uselessness and not necessarily their destruction is being emphasized. He is not threatening them with Hell but is lifting them (encouraging) them to a place of productivity and fruitfulness.

USELESS BRANCHES THROWN OUT

How will the world know, if we are attached to the vine? As the world watches our lives, what fruit will they see? Messiah gave us a vivid example of how to communicate to the world that we are truly His disciples, attached to the Vine, and producing the fruit that reflects His character.

> John 13:34 —A new commandment I give to you, that you love one another, even as I have loved you, that you also love one another. By this all men will know that you are My disciples, if you have love for one another.

This love will be the testimony to convince all men that our faith is genuine. This testimony of love was displayed by Jim Elliot and his companions who dedicated their lives to reaching the Auca Indians with the Good News of Jesus. Although I was moved by the accounts that I read of what happened to them, the recently released movie, *The End of the Spear* captivated me and made me think just how these ordinary men bore fruit to the pagan world that they entered. They were a testimony to these Auca Indians, who only knew a savage, fearful lifestyle of killing not only their enemies, but also each other. Even though Jim and his companions gave their lives for the sake of the Gospel, the sweet savor of the fruit of love continues to impact the Auca community today. One of Jim Elliot's famous quotes is: "He is no fool to give up what he cannot keep to gain what he cannot lose." Truly, Jim and the other men with him, were abiding in the Vine and the impact of their testimony remains.

On the other hand, if a believer is not abiding in the Lord and trying to live independently from the Vine, there are consequences for not abiding. By living apart from the vine we are dishonoring the Lord. The fruit we bear brings disgrace to God instead of a testimony to the grace of God.

To those in the world who are observing our behavior, if we are not bearing fruit as we go through real life situations, then our witness becomes useless, to be thrown out in the trash and burned up. Each of us can probably think of our own illustrations, when a high profile minister or believer disgraces the name of the Lord, through financial impropriety or even sexual promiscuity, or just being unloving. What happens to the impact to the world around them? Their testimony is useless, nothing but fuel for the burning.

GOOD FOR FUEL ONLY

Ezekiel 15:1-7a —Then the word of the Lord came to me saying, "Son of man, how is the wood of the vine better than any wood of a branch which is among the trees of the forest? Can wood be taken from it to make anything, or can men take a peg from it on which to hang any vessel? If it has been put into the fire for fuel, and the fire has consumed both of its ends, and its middle part has been charred, is it then useful for anything? Behold, while it is intact, it is not made into anything. How much less, when the fire has consumed it and it is charred, can it still be made into anything! Therefore, thus says the Lord God, 'As the wood of the vine among the trees of the forest, which I have given to the fire for fuel, so have I given up the inhabitants of Jerusalem; and I set My face against them.

This portion is stressing that the wood of the vine is useless except for fulfilling the vine's proper function, the production of grapes. The wood of the dead vine branch cannot be used to make a coffee table or even used as a peg to hang something on. It is only to be thrown into the fire and burned.

If the branch is not abiding in the vine to produce fruit, it will be rendered useless. There are many believers who choose not to abide, but rather to live a carnal life that grieves the heart of God. The relationship is still there, but the intimacy and the potential fruitfulness is lost. The fruit of God's Spirit like love, joy, peace, lovingkindness, and patience are not there and there is nothing to attract those who are watching and desiring to find the reality of God's love. The purpose of our lives is to represent God and live out His character in the fruit that we bear, so those who are desperate to find answers for their lives will see the reality and meaningfulness of having a relationship with the living God.

It may be easy for us to point a finger at a high profile believer who brings disgrace to the honor of God, but the same principle holds true for you and me. This is why Messiah was imploring His disciples to remember that if they attempt to bear fruit without abiding in Him, then all that they will produce will be useless, branches that are only good for burning. Messiah wants us to continually realize that to abide in Him, means an active condition of remaining, or sticking like glue to the Vine.

Peter learned that when he was abiding in Messiah, then he was the Peter that God intended him to be. His full potential was realized when he was in his Master's presence. Even fishing worked out well.

HE IS THE BEST IN ME

As a part of an assignment for a doctoral thesis, a college student spent a year with a group of Navajo Indians on a reservation in the Southwest. As he did his research he lived with one family, sleeping in their hut, eating their food, working with them, and generally living the life of a twentieth-century Indian.

The old grandmother of the family spoke no English at all, yet a very close friendship formed between the two. They spent a great deal of time sharing a friendship that was meaningful to each, yet unexplainable to anyone else. In spite of the language difference, they shared the common language of love and understood each other. Over the months he learned a few phrases of Navajo, and she picked up a little of the English language. When it was time for him to return to the campus and write his thesis, the tribe held a going-away celebration. It was marked by sadness since the young man had become close to the whole village and all would miss him.

As he prepared to get into the pickup truck and leave, the old grandmother came to tell him goodbye. With tears streaming from her eyes, she placed her hands on either side of his face, looked directly into his eyes and said, "I like me best when I'm with you." Isn't that the way we feel in the presence of Yeshua? He brings out the best in us. We learn to see ourselves as worthy and valuable when we are in His presence. The hurts, the cares, the disappointments of our lives are behind us when we look in His eyes and realize the depth of His love.

Our self-esteem no longer depends on what we have done or failed to do; it depends only on the value that He places on us. To be conformed to the image of Messiah is to generate in other people the Indian grandmother's simple statement: "I like me best when I'm with you." I like me the best when I abide in my Beloved. He brings out the best in me, He is the best in me.

We like ourselves the best when we recognize that Messiah gives us His esteem, His value, and His eternal purpose. There is no better place to be, than to be attached to the vine, being nourished by His life, and cleansed by His Word anticipating the greater harvest and feast that follows.

THOUGHT QUESTIONS AND REFLECTIONS:

1. Review what it means for Messiah to be the true vine and for His Father to be the vinedresser.

2. Describe the process of abiding in the vine.

3. How did Messiah lift Peter up when Peter denied Him?

4. Describe the occasion Yeshua utilized to confirm Peter's
    calling to service and think about how the Lord has
    worked in your own life to confirm his plan for you.

5. Discuss the difference between pruning and having the
    useless branches thrown out.

These things I have spoken to you, that My joy may be in you, and that your joy may be made full.

John 15:11

Chapter 4

A Life of Significance

Joyful Assurance

*H*ave you ever applied for a job with a Fortune 500 company? Once the position is granted, you might be anxious to review that impressive benefits package that was promised, which included a lucrative salary, health insurance, vacation, and a retirement savings plan. For most of us a package like this is only a dream. However, there is no need to despair, for the benefits of abiding in Messiah surpass beyond measure all the rewards this world can present. The success measured by God is dynamically superior to what the best earthly company could ever offer.

John 15:7-11 lays out the benefits that result from abiding in Him, including: answered prayer, complete joy, and a unique relationship with the CEO of the universe, just to name a few. Let us take a deeper look at the word joy in the context of the Hebrew Scriptures.

WHAT IS JOY?

Choosing the perfect name for a new baby can be both an adventure and a wonderful time of creativity. In Jewish family life, selecting a name is very important, as it often ties into tradition and the family's expectation. For baby boys, the name is officially given eight days after birth at his circumcision. My husband Sam is from an Ashkenazi Jewish family, which means his relatives emigrated from Eastern Europe. In the Ashkenazi tradition children are usually named after a deceased relative to honor their memory. When our first son was born we wanted to honor Sam's mother, Jean, so we took the letter J and named our son Joshua.

Oftentimes parents pick a name hoping that it will be reflected in the baby's personality as the child grows. In Biblical times, children were given names that represented a truth about them or about God.

For example, Samuel means heard of God and reminded Hannah that God heard her request for a son (1 Samuel 1). Today it is common for parents to choose Scriptural names. For instance, our son's first name, Joshua means God is salvation and his middle name, Abraham means father of many nations.

I have always loved names that reflect the qualities of the Lord, like Grace and Joy. In fact, I can think of three

Hebrew names meaning joy that are common in Israel today. One of the names is Simcha, which means mirth or gladness and has the idea of celebration. *Simcha* is found in a number of verses such as Psalm 16:11 where it says,

> You will show me the path of life; in Your presence is fullness of joy [*simcha*]; at Your right hand are pleasures forevermore.

When my Israeli friend gave birth to a girl, she named her, Roni. I discovered from the Hebrew dictionary that Roni comes from the root *ranan*, which means to give a shout for joy or sing for joy.

> Isaiah 12:6 —Cry aloud and shout for joy [*roni*], O inhabitants of Zion, for great in your midst is the Holy One of Israel.

Gila is another beautiful Hebrew name that is common in Israel today and means to rejoice, to cry out, and to exult. One portion where *gila* is used twice is found in Isaiah 35:1, and describes rejoicing because of new life in the barren places,

> "The wilderness and the desert will be glad [*gil*], and the Arabah will rejoice [*gil*] and blossom.

From these three different words for joy: *simcha, roni* and *gila* we learn various aspects of what it means to live joyfully according to the Scriptures. The idea of *simcha* teaches us that when we are in the presence of the Lord we will have complete delight with full pleasure in our celebrations. Moreover, in God's appointment calendar with Israel (Leviticus 23) there are commands to celebrate and be joyful throughout as we meet together to worship the Lord. From *roni* we learn that when the Holy One of Israel is in your midst, it is time to celebrate through exuberant worship. When God is in our midst, it is worth singing and shouting with joyful enthusiasm.

Gila is similar to *roni*, and emphasizes the idea to cry out and to glory in. We find the usage of *gila* in Isaiah, where in the coming Kingdom, God will cause the desert to flourish. The King of kings will make all things new. What a great reason to rejoice and be glad as we eagerly anticipate the time when sorrow and sadness will flee away and we will be living in the reality of our eternal home.

REJOICE ALWAYS?

I look forward to that time when all tears will be wiped away and I believe that then I will be able to experience perpetual joy. However, meantime back on planet earth, it is just not all that simple to be joyful always. Nonetheless, the Scriptures are clear that having joy is a vital part of our walk of faith. Messiah during His teaching after the Passover meal exhorted His disciples,

> John 15:11 —These things I have spoken to you, that My joy may be in you, and that your joy may be made full.

Paul also encouraged the congregation in Philippi,

> Philippians 4:4 —Rejoice in the Lord always, and again I say rejoice.

Finding perfect joy and continuing to rejoice at all times does not seem very natural for me. I tend to be more pessimistic, rather than optimistic. Just recently I got sick and completely lost my voice. I could barely whisper. I had shared with my friend, perhaps a little boastfully, that even though I regularly speak and sing, I have strong vocal chords and don't have to worry about losing my voice. So now that my voice is gone, I felt that God might be chastising me. In my pessimism I am writing out messages on a pad in order to communicate with others and wondering what's next. I am thinking and praying,

> Lord, have I taken You for granted? I would really like to have my voice back and be at full capacity, but help me to have your perspective on this situation. I know that You don't need me to be teaching and singing as much as you desire my obedience to follow Your will and my heart to be pure. Help me to have "the joy of the LORD as my strength."

HOW CAN HIS JOY BE MY STRENGTH?

The phrase "the joy of the LORD is your strength" is found in Nehemiah 8:10b and may even be familiar to you. Let us take a look at it in the context of Scripture. A number of Israelites who had been in the exile because of the Babylonian captivity were returning to Jerusalem. Sadly the walls around Jerusalem were broken down leaving the city vulnerable and unprotected from attacks. Through the perseverance of Nehemiah's leadership and with the help of some faithful Israelites the walls of Jerusalem had just been rebuilt (Nehemiah 6:15-16).

In Nehemiah chapter eight we have all the people gathered to observe the Fall Feasts of Israel, which included the Feast of Tabernacles. Ezra, the priest and the Levites brought the Hebrew Scrolls and began reading, from the early morning until the middle of the day.

Nehemiah 8:8 —They read from the book, from the law of God, translating to give the sense so that they understood the reading.

As the people understood the Word of God it did not result in celebration, but rather in weeping and mourning over their sense of sinfulness.

PIERCING JOY

The inhabitants of Jerusalem were being drawn back to God as the Word of God was penetrating through their hearts and souls. They had gone into exile because of their disobedience and even though they returned to the Land, they had not come back to the Lord. God's Holy Word was cutting through their apathy and waywardness. However, after being convicted by the Scriptures, they were desirous to follow the Lord with all their heart, soul, and might.

Nevertheless, instead of letting them grieve over their sins, Nehemiah gives them rather a strange admonition:

Nehemiah 8:10 —Go, eat of the fat, drink of the sweet, and send portions to him who has nothing prepared; for this day is holy to our Lord. Do not be grieved, for the joy of the LORD is your strength.

First, Nehemiah tells them to eat party food. Celebrate with yummy treats and if your neighbors don't have any food ready then send some goodies to them so they can rejoice as well. The Hebrew word *kee* means for or because and gives us two reasons to have a festive time with scrumptious eats and drinks.

1. For [because] this day is holy to the Lord this celebration is about God and glorifying Him. God was telling them to take time apart as sacred, *kadosh,* holy unto the Lord and to celebrate His goodness.

2. For [because] the joy of the LORD is your strength. The Hebrew word for joy is *chedvah* and has the idea of sharp, piercing joy. Since this joy belongs to the LORD it will bring you God's perspective on what is happening around you.

It's like driving out early in the morning in a dense fog, barely being able to see the road, but as the sun begins to shine brighter and brighter the fog burns off and you can see the road ahead that was always there, but now is clearly revealed. Often we cannot understand or see the outcome for certain situations, but as we find that the joy of the Lord is our strength, then in turn, He gives us His heavenly perspective to see our lives and our circumstances in light of eternity.

His joy can pierce through the pain, the confusion and show us that He is indeed the Way, the Truth and the Life. Romans 8:28 can become a daily reality as we testify that all things are working together for good to those who love Him and are called according to His purposes.

Note that this joy is from our covenant-making God, the LORD. His perspective on my life is my strength. Strength in Hebrew is *maoz* and means not only strength but also a place of safety, protection, and refuge. In other words, His strength is a stronghold that will give us His Divine haven as we face the storms of life.

When the joy of the Lord is your power you are strengthened to celebrate and you can encourage those around you to rejoice as well.

CHEER UP ALREADY

Have you ever been depressed or felt discouraged and a friend comes along and tries to encourage you by saying, "Hey, snap out of it, cheer up, things can't be that bad." Now this might be a well meaning friend who just does not have a grasp on the situation that you are in. This friend has never experienced the depths of despair that you are facing. Therefore she may be well meaning in her attempt to cheer you up but her words have little effect on you and your ability to cope with the situation.

On the other hand suppose a loving caring friend came by and saw your despair and your need to have a different perspective about your current circumstance. This friend not only understood what you were going through but had been through a very similar situation and had immerged victorious. If this same friend encouraged you by saying, "Cheer up because I have been where you have been and I know that the Lord is with you and He surely will bring you through." Would you be willing to listen and believe this friend?

There is one more friend for you to consider. This friend sticks closer that a brother. He is the One who told His followers that if they stuck close to Him like glue, their joy would be full. If your beloved Messiah told you to cheer up and trust Him in the midst of a situation, how would you respond? Let's look at one of the places where Messiah commands His followers to "cheer up and take courage!"

In other words, when Messiah gives this command He is in effect encouraging us to let His joy be our strength.

JOY IN THE MIDST OF TEMPEST

In the book of Matthew we read that Messiah tries to get away from the crowds by getting into a boat, He then finds a more isolated place, He finds Himself followed by throngs of people from the cities. Being filled with compassion Messiah took time to minister to them and healed the sick. It was getting late and Yeshua realized that there was no place to eat so from the sacrificial lunch of five loaves and two fishes He miraculously feeds five thousand men plus the women and children.

The Scriptures say that immediately after this Messiah tells His disciples to get in a boat and go ahead of Him to the other side of the sea of Galilee. Yeshua stays behind by the mountain to be alone and to pray but then He sees that a storm has arisen and that the disciples were being tossed about by the winds and the rough sea.

Matthew 14:24-33 —The boat was already a considerable distance from land, buffeted by the waves because the wind was against it. And in the fourth watch of the night He came to them, walking on the sea. And when the disciples saw Him walking on the sea, they were frightened, saying, "It is a ghost!" And they cried out for fear. But immediately Yeshua spoke to them, saying, "Take courage, it is I; do not be afraid." And Peter answered Him and said, "Lord, if it is You, command me to come to You on the water." And He said, "Come!" And Peter got out of the boat, and walked on the water and came toward Jesus. But seeing the wind, he became afraid, and beginning to sink, he cried out, saying, "Lord, save me!" And immediately Yeshua stretched out His hand and took hold of him, and said to him, "O you of little faith, why did you doubt?" And when they got into the boat, the wind stopped. And those who were in the boat worshiped Him, saying, "You are certainly God's Son!"

Here we have this famous scene where Messiah comes to them walking on the water. The disciples think he is a ghost but what does Messiah say to them, "Be of good cheer, take courage, it is I, do not be afraid." His command cuts through the storm and danger and He tells them to have His joy and courage and to not be afraid because He has the authority and power over this storm. The disciples were terrified. Peter had stepped out on the raging sea approaching Yeshua. He was doing really well as he walked even as on dry land until he took His focus off the Lord and turned his eyes to the hostile wind. Then Peter began to sink. Even though his Beloved Master was just a few feet away it was not enough, Peter had to be focused on the Lord and not on the storm. Likewise in my personal life I often mistakenly pray, "O Lord, I am giving this storm to you." Then I open my eyes and focus on the storm and not the Lord in the midst of the storm.

HIS JOY IS COMPLETE IN YOU

John 15:11—These things I have spoken to you, that My joy may be in you, and that your joy may be made full.

The path to find joy in the midst of any situation is to realize that Messiah is already victorious and His strength is the answer for you. What storms are in your life? Is there something that is swirling around you, and you feel like the disciples who were in the flimsy boat, about to be thrown overboard by the violent winds of your situation? Don't take your eyes off your Beloved. The answer lies in your abiding in Him. As we entrust each situation to our Covenant God we will find His joy to be our only strength.

ANSWERED PRAYER

John 15:7-8 —If you abide in Me, and My words abide in you, ask whatever you wish, and it shall be done for you. By this is My Father glorified, that you bear much fruit, and so prove to be My disciples.

To qualify for answered prayer we must choose to live dependently upon God. When we abide in Messiah, His teaching will permeate our minds and hearts. As a result our lives will radiate the joy of the Lord, and those around us will see that our God is able to meet all our needs and hear our prayers. The fruit of our lives displays the likeness of God manifested through the fruit of the Spirit (Galatians 5:22). The witness of answered prayer testifies to those who are watching that we serve a loving, caring Father. As others see us give praise to God for what He alone can do, then perhaps they will desire to taste for themselves and see that the Lord is good.

MOTIVATED BY LOVE

John 15:9-10 —Just as the Father has loved Me, I have also loved you; abide in My love. If you keep My commandments, you will abide in My love; just as I have kept My Father's commandments, and abide in His love.

God is the source of all love, all compassion, all kindness and affection. God's perfect love will cast out every fear (John 10:30, 1 John 4:18). Messiah is inviting us to continue in His love; in order to do so, we need to abide in His love. How can we know that we are abiding in His love? The evidence will be seen in our obedience to His Word.

As we grow deeper in our understanding of God's infinite love for us, this obedience will be born out of our appreciation for God, not out of obligation. In Messiah's earthly ministry He gave us the perfect example of obedience to emulate. Yeshua did all things out of love for His Father, and only what was pleasing to Him (John 8:29).

Messiah gives His followers a further explanation of His love, where He no longer calls them slaves, but rather His friends. This friendship provides a greater level of intimacy as Messiah explains what true friends do for each other (John 15:12-17). Likewise, we are Messiah's friends just like Abraham, Moses and David. May our lives be motivated by His love as we live confidently for Him, and bear much fruit to glorify Him.

ASSURANCE OF HIS COVENANT LOVE

Our God is a Covenant God. From the beginning of creation, God initiated His relationship with man through the covenants. God takes covenants very seriously. Even man-made covenants provide some measure of security.

Understanding God's covenant love changed my life. The biblical account of Mephibosheth clearly portrays how a covenant relationship brings security and restoration.

> 2 Samuel 4:4 —Now Jonathan, Saul's son, had a son crippled in his feet. He was five years old when the report of Saul and Jonathan came from Jezreel, and his nurse took him up and fled. And it happened that in her hurry to flee, he fell and became lame. And his name was Mephibosheth.

Mephibosheth was born into the royal family. His father was Jonathan, son of the first king of Israel, Saul. He had a great future ahead of him until tragedy struck.

At the age of five, Mephibosheth's father and grandfather died in battle and he became a possible heir to Saul's throne. When the news arrived, fear gripped the household.

SAFE ESCAPE

They had to flee. David would surely take over now that Saul and Jonathan were out of the way. David had been anointed by Samuel, and the enmity between Saul and David was a known fact. Logic dictated that David would clear his path to the throne. The Scriptures do not tell us exactly what was on their minds; we know only that the news of the tragedy was enough to send them fleeing from their home.

Little Mephibosheth's nurse "took him up" and fled. In all the confusion and horror, the child fell and became lame. Mephibosheth would now be crippled for the rest of his life. He was taken to live in Lo-devar. In fact, the name of the city meant "no pasture"… a barren, unsightly place across the Jordan River. He was a prince without a throne, his inheritance lost, and no doubt lived in fear for his life.

UNEXPECTED INVITATION

One day king David asked Mephibosheth to appear before him in Jerusalem. The Scripture reveals that Mephibosheth had no idea why he had been summoned. Not knowing what to expect, he anticipated the worst.

> 2 Samuel 9:5-8 —Then King David sent and brought him from the house of Machir the son of Ammiel, from Lo-debar. Mephibosheth, the son of Jonathan the son of Saul, came to David and fell on his face and prostrated himself. And David said, "Mephibosheth." And he said, "Here is your servant!" David said to him, "Do not fear, for I will surely show kindness to you for the sake of your father Jonathan, and will restore to you all the land of your grandfather Saul; and you shall eat at my table regularly." Again he prostrated himself and said, "What is your servant, that you should regard a dead dog like me?"

COVENANT LOVE AT WORK

The Hebrew expression "dead dog" was used for someone contemptible or useless. That is how Mephibosheth saw himself. But David, a man after God's own heart, sought to show kindness to Mephibosheth. Why? Because a covenant was cut on behalf of Mephibosheth between David and Jonathan. The word "kindness" in Hebrew is *hesed*, which means loyal, covenant love. Note that David's motivation for showing kindness to Mephibosheth was not pity for the crippled man, but rather David's desire to honor Jonathan, the father. What he did, he did "for Jonathan's sake." Honoring the promise of the covenant that he made with Jonathan. Here we see the heart of the covenant that provided security, protection, and fulfillment.

> 1 Samuel 20:14-17 —If I am still alive, will you not show me the lovingkindness [*hesed*] of the LORD, that I may not die? You shall not cut off your lovingkindness [*hesed*] from my [Jonathan's] house forever, not even when the LORD cuts off every one of the enemies of David from the face of the earth." So Jonathan made a covenant with the house of David, saying, "May the LORD require it at the hands of David's enemies. Jonathan made David vow again because of his love for him, because he loved him as he loved his own life."

LOVE IS A ROOT OF THE COVENANT

Jonathan made a covenant with David because of his love for David. Jonathan loved David as he loved his own life. If Saul's household had known about the covenant between David and Jonathan, much fear could have been avoided. Mephibosheth would not have become crippled nor would he have had to live in a desolate and barren place. Furthermore, the king of Israel said to Mephibosheth,

> 2 Samuel 9:7 —Do not fear, for I will surely show kindness to you for the sake of your father Jonathan, and will restore to you all the land of your grandfather Saul; and you shall eat at my table regularly.

Mephibosheth is a picture of the redeemed sinner, called into the King's presence, fully restored to the royal fellowship, protected and given a glorious inheritance. God wants to do the same for you. In some way each of us can relate to this story. Even though we may not be lame nor live in a barren place, we may have a heart that is crippled, a soul that is lonely, or live in fear of our past, present, and future. Maybe we feel like a failure...hopeless, unloved and without purpose. That's how I felt. But deep in my heart I longed for unconditional love, acceptance, and sense of belonging. Then one day, I learned of a covenant made on my behalf called a New Covenant.

Just like Mephibosheth, I am a redeemed sinner. Through Yeshua I have access to God's presence, protected by His grace, and granted an eternal inheritance.

> Ephesians 1:3-12 —Blessed be the God and Father of our Lord Jesus the Messiah, who has blessed us with every spiritual blessing in the heavenly places in Messiah, just as He chose us in Him before the foundation of the world, that we should be holy and blameless before Him. In love He predestined us to adoption as sons through Jesus the Messiah to Himself, according to the kind intention of His will, to the praise of the glory of His grace, which He freely bestowed on us in the Beloved. In Him we have redemption through His blood, the forgiveness of our trespasses, according to the riches of His grace, which He lavished upon us. In all wisdom and insight He made known to us the mystery of His will, according to His kind intention which He purposed in Him with a view to an administration suitable to the fullness of the times, that is, the summing up of all things in, things in the heavens and things upon the earth. In Him also we

have obtained an inheritance, having been predestined according to His purpose who works all things after the counsel of His will, to the end that we who were the first to hope in Messiah should be to the praise of His glory.

God knows our need for security, significance and intimacy. Just as David made a covenant with Jonathan because of his love, devotion and friendship, so Messiah also made a covenant with His friends. This New Covenant will secure their relationship forever. He not only cut the covenant on our behalf, but also was cut as a covenant sacrifice. We do have a written contract as a testimony of God's covenant with us. We have His love letters to us in His inspired Word of God.

The process of covenant making reveals the blessings that are accompanied with each step. As adapted from the book, *Our Covenant God* by Kay Arthur, the process of making a covenant will deepen our appreciation of the provisions and blessings the covenant provides. Let us carefully consider each step, by applying Scripture to our lives.

THE PROCESS OF CUTTING A COVENANT

The animals had been slain-cut in half down the spine. Their bright blood stained the stones, the dirt, the grass, with sprinkles of wildflowers in their display of color. A covenant was being cut. The two parties stand opposite one another. Each removed their own robes and handed over to each other, then each clothed himself in his covenant's brother garment.

I am putting on your clothes ....and you are putting on mine. We are one.

Before we entered into covenant with God we have to understand what our garments were like as described in Isaiah 64:6,

> For all of us have become like one who is unclean, And all our righteous deeds are like a filthy garment; And all of us wither like a leaf, And our iniquities, like the wind, take us away.

But when we come into a covenant relationship with our God, He removes our old sinful garments and we receive His garments of salvation.

> Isaiah 61:10 —I will rejoice greatly in the LORD, My soul will exult in my God; For He has clothed me with garments of salvation, He has wrapped me with a robe of righteousness, As a bridegroom decks himself with a garland, And as a bride adorns herself with her jewels.

> Galatians 3:27 —For all of you who were baptized into Messiah have clothed yourselves with Messiah.

Picking up their weapons from the ground, each hands the other his sword, his bow. By this action they understood...

Your enemies are now mine... mine are yours.

Our covenant God takes our weapons of the flesh and replaces them with His armor, His protection.

> Romans 12:19 —Never take your own revenge,

beloved, but leave room for the wrath of God, for it is written, "Vengeance is Mine, I will repay," says the Lord.

We realize that we are in a different kind of a battle this side of heaven. We are truly one with the Lord and need to dress ourselves in the armor of God.

2 Corinthians 10:3-5 — For though we walk in the flesh, we do not war according to the flesh, for the weapons of our warfare are not of the flesh, but divinely powerful for the destruction of fortresses. We are destroying speculations and every lofty thing raised up against the knowledge of God, and we are taking every thought captive to the obedience of Messiah.

Like King David we can pray to God, "Contend, O LORD, with those who contend with me; fight against those who fight against me" (Psalm 35:1).

Psalm 56:3-4 —When I am afraid, I will put my trust in Thee. 4 In God, whose word I praise, In God I have put my trust; I shall not be afraid. What can mere man do to me?

Then they handed each other their belt declaring:
"When you are weak, my strength will be there for you."

As we enter into covenant with our God, we recognize that He surely understands our weaknesses. This is why He is our source of strength. As we trust in Him, He makes us strong.

Psalm 103:14 —For He Himself knows our frame; He is mindful that we are but dust.

Philippians 4:13 —I can do all things through Him who strengthens me.

Psalm 28:7 —The LORD is my strength and my shield; My heart trusts in Him, and I am helped; Therefore my heart exults, And with my song I shall thank Him.

It was customary in the Middle East as part of making a covenant to swear by the oath. First they pointed to heaven and said, "God do so to me..." following this they pointed to the slain animals, saying, "If I break this covenant then it will be done to me as to these animals." In other words, to break a covenant meant to lose a life. Then each party made a cut on his wrist, and with a handclap, the two men mingled their blood declaring:

What is mine is yours...what is yours is mine.

In this section we must recognize that because the covenant is dependent on what God alone can provide, He has given us an unbreakable covenant because it is cut in Messiah's own blood.

Genesis 15:17-18a —And it came about when the sun had set, that it was very dark, and behold, there appeared a smoking oven and a flaming torch which passed between these pieces. On that day the LORD made a covenant with Abram"

Hebrews 6:17-18 -In the same way God, desiring even more to show to the heirs of the promise the unchangeableness of His purpose, interposed with an oath, in order that by two unchangeable things, in which it is impossible for God to lie, we may have strong encouragement, we who have fled for refuge in laying hold of the hope set before us.

Each reached down and scooped up dirt mingled with small stones and rubbed his abrasive into the cut in his wrist.

Wherever I am, when I lift my hand and see the scar, I will remember I have a covenant partner.

As we consider what Messiah has done on our behalf to secure the New Covenant we need to trust in His finished work of atonement for us. His scars are visible in His resurrected body.

John 20:26-28 —And after eight days again His disciples were inside, and Thomas with them. Jesus came, the doors having been shut, and stood in their midst, and said, "Peace be with you." Then He said to Thomas, "Reach here your finger, and see My hands; and reach here your hand, and put it into My side; and be not unbelieving, but believing." Thomas answered and said to Him, "My Lord and my God!"

The next important step in the process was the exchange of their names. Then they said to each other,

Because of the covenant I have a new identity

2 Corinthians 5:17 —Therefore, if anyone is in Messiah he is a new creation; the old has gone, the new has come!

109

Luke 10:20b —Rejoice that your names are recorded in heaven.

Revelation 2:17—To him who overcomes, to him I will give some of the hidden manna, and I will give him a white stone, and a new name written on the stone which no one knows but he who receives it.'

Revelation 3:5 —He who overcomes shall thus be clothed in white garments; and I will not erase his name from the book of life, and I will confess his name before My Father, and before His angels.

The cutting of a covenant always includes a fellowship meal. One broke bread and placed it in the covenant partner's mouth; then the other did the same. Together they said,

You are eating with me, and I with you

Revelation 19:9 —And he said to me, "Write, 'Blessed are those who are invited to the marriage supper of the Lamb.'" And he said to me, "These are true words of God."

Revelation 3:20 —Behold, I stand at the door and knock; if anyone hears My voice and opens the door, I will come in to him, and will dine with him, and he with Me.

Finally a memorial was set up: a pile of stones, a planted tree and a written contract as a testimony of the covenant they had made.

*Now I call you Friend — my Friend who sticks
closer than a brother.*

Proverbs 18:24b —There is a friend who sticks closer
than a brother.

John 15:14-15 —You are My friends, if you do what I
command you. No longer do I call you slaves, for the
slave does not know what his master is doing; but I have
called you friends, for all things that I have heard from
My Father I have made known to you.

James 2:23 —And Abraham believed God, and it was
reckoned to him as righteousness," and he was called
the friend of God.

Just like Abraham and Moses were friends of God, we,
too, through the New Covenant, can speak to our Beloved
as our closest friend and confidant.

You have been created to love Him, to adore Him, and
to be loved by Him. Let us never underestimate the power
of His redeeming love. For He not only cut a covenant
on your behalf, but also He was cut for your sins. You no
longer have to live in fear of your past, present or future.

Let us live as citizens of His Kingdom and represent the
King of kings. May this world see that there is a Redeemer,
and there is security in His covenant love.

THOUGHT QUESTIONS AND REFLECTIONS:

1. Review the various meanings for joy in the Scriptures and discuss how these concepts add to our celebrations as we meet with the Lord.

2. Discuss what it means for the joy of the LORD to be your strength.

3. Consider times in your own life when the Lord has encouraged you to "cheer up and be of good courage."

4. Reflect on answers to prayer where the Lord has been glorified as a testimony to those who are watching you.

5. Think about your Beloved and thank Him for the security, significance and intimacy His covenant has brought to your life.

Bibliography

Arthur, Kay, *Our Covenant God*, Water Brook Press, 2003

Bingham, Dottie, *Grace for the Rest of Your Life*, Gracestoration, 1990

Boa, Kenneth, *Conformed to His Image*, Zondervan, 2001

Bruce, F. F., *The Gospel of John*, Eerdmans Publishing Company, 1983

Dean, Robert Jr. and Ice, Thomas, *What Bible Teaches About Spiritual Warfare*, Kregel Publications, 1990

Derickson, Gary and Radmacher, Earl, *The Disciplemaker*, Charis Press, 2001

Edersheim, Alferd, *The Life and Times of Jesus the Messiah*, MacDonald Publishing Company

Leupold, H. C., *Exposition of Isaiah*, Baker Book House, 1981

MacArthur John, *The MacArthur New Testament Commentary Ephesians*, Moody Press, 1986

Morris, Leon, *The Gospel According to John*, Eerdmans Publishing Company, 1971

Oswalt, John N., *The Book of Isaiah Chapters 1-39*, Eerdmans Publishing Company,1986

Pink, A. W., *Gleanings in Genesis*, Moody Press, 1976

Rosten, Leo, *The Joys of Yiddish*, McGraw-Hill Book Company, 1968

Tenney, Merrill C., *John, The Gospel of Belief,* Eerdmans Publishing Company, 1948

Wiersbe, Warren W., *Be Rich*, Victor Books, 1986

Zlotowitz, Meir, *The ArtScroll Tanach Series on Beresishes*, Mesorah Publications, 1986

Resources by
Word of Messiah Ministries

Messianic Foundations: Fulfill Your Calling in the Jewish Messiah - offers a vision of the Messianic Movement motivated by the testimony that Yeshua is God's faithfulness to Israel.

Messiah in the Feasts of Israel - This shows how the Feasts supernaturally and Biblically point to Messiah.

Messianic Discipleship: Following Yeshua, Growing in Messiah - leads the reader through a Jewish discipleship course, dealing with the essentials of Messianic faith.

The Messianic Answer Book - answers to the 15 most asked questions Jewish people have about the faith. Excellent tool for sharing with those seeking answers.

Even You Can Share The Jewish Messiah - a short booklet with key information on sharing Yeshua with friends and neighbors, even "to the Jew first" (Romans 1:16).

The Messianic Passover Haggadah - the perfect guide for conducting your own Passover Seder.

Messianic Wisdom: Practical Scriptural Answers for Your Life - get a grasp on Messianic Jewish issues and living out your faith in Messiah. Essential and inspiring, this book is for every growing disciple of Yeshua.

Messianic Life Lessons from the Book of Jonah - do you want to know God's will for your life? Jonah proves that this alone will not help! A slender commentary on this book about Israel's mission to the Gentiles.

Honoring God with My Life: Issues of Sense and Sensibility - This discipleship book for women is meant not only to help you to grow and mature in qualities from Titus 2:3-5, but to equip you to mentor and disciple other women. 232 Pages.

Abiding in Messiah

by Miriam Nadler

© *2011 by Miriam Nadler*
All Rights Reserved
Printed in United States of America
ISBN: 9781519294708

Made in the USA
Lexington, KY
03 September 2017